GUERRILLA MARKETING FIELD GUIDE

30

POWERFUL BATTLE MANEUVERS FOR NON-STOP MOMENTUM AND RESULTS

JAY CONRAD LEVINSON
AND JEANNIE LEVINSON

Ep
Entrepreneur
PRESS®

Entrepreneur Press, Publisher
Cover design: Andrew Welyczko
Composition and production: Eliot House Productions

This publication is designed to provide accurate and authoritative
information in regard to the subject matter covered. It is sold with the
understanding that the publisher is not engaged in rendering legal,
accounting, or other professional services. If legal advice or other expert
assistance is required, the services of a competent professional person
should be sought.

Library of Congress Cataloging-in-Publication Data
Levinson, Jay Conrad.
    Guerrilla marketing field guide: 30 powerful battle maneuvers
for non-stop momentum and results / by Jay Conrad Levinson.
        p. cm.
    ISBN-13: 978-1-59918-453-1 (alk. paper)
    ISBN-10: 1-59918-453-2 (alk. paper)
    1. Marketing. 2. Strategic planning. I. Title.
HF5415.L47618 2013
658.8–dc23   2012032842

Printed in the United States of America

17 16 15 14 13   10 9 8 7 6 5 4 3 2 1

DEDICATION

*To our brilliant master trainers—who teach the world how to win
battles and profits with guerrilla marketing:*

Frank Adkins (FLORIDA)

Teo Alexsov (MACEDONIA)

Bob Bare (TEXAS)

Dobbin Buck (GEORGIA)

Soesh Chadda (INDIA)

Ken Chee (CHINA)

Patrick Cumiskey (IRELAND)

Bruce Doyle (AUSTRALIA)

David T. Fagan
(WASHINGTON)

Andrea Fausin (ITALY)

Al Garlick (NEW YORK)

Lee Goff (GEORGIA)

Paul R. J. Hanley
(deceased) (ENGLAND)

Daniel Jeremy Huffman
(FLORIDA)

Alexandru Israil (ROMANIA)

Art Lee (CALIFORNIA)

Larry Loebig (CALIFORNIA)

Kelvin Lim Kian Meng
(SINGAPORE)

Dr. Kim Marie (FLORIDA)

Peter Nehr (FLORIDA)

Dr. Azizan Osman
(MALAYSIA)

Paulo Pereiro (BRAZIL)

A. J. Perishko (IOWA)

Barry Plasko (ISRAEL)

William Reed (JAPAN)

Ravi Sood (CANADA)

Helen Stevens (ENGLAND)

Wendy Stevens (TENNESSEE)

Dan Storey (ENGLAND)

Lin Tan (SINGAPORE)

Michael Tasner (NEW YORK)

Eric Villerama (PHILIPPINES)

Mike Warren (COLORADO)

Dr. W.B. (Bill) Williams, DMD.
(GEORGIA)

Todd Woods (ARIZONA)

CONTENTS

★

V

PART II
AFTER THE BATTLE

PART III
APPENDICES

Contents

ACKNOWLEDGMENTS

(alphabetical)

★

Ginger & Frank Adkins

Ratan & Karuna Ahuja

Cheryl Allen

Eve Bauchard

Karen Billipp

Debbie Billingsley

Dawn Byrk

Jere Calmes

Carolyn Evans

Natalie Farber

Leanne Harvey

Chris Hood

Susan Howell

Christy Huffman

Jeremy & Sami Huffman

Joshua Huffman

Melanie Pas Ingham

Shrish Kalla

Phil Kaprow

Samantha Knowles

Gary Krebs

Amy Levinson

Rebecca Levy

Alan List

Christine Malone

Mohamad Masri

Ruth Matti

Jillian McTigue

Rhonda Pagan

Loie & Rick Polanski

Sharon Sands

Latisha Sorce

Cheryl Smith

Barbara Swims

Sierra Theodore

Karen Thomas

Courtney Thurman

John & Julie Von Aken

Wade Vose

Chris Walls

Ron Young

Acknowledgments

PART

I

THE
MISSION

CHAPTER 1

ADVANCING INTO BATTLE

★

EVEN IF YOU KNEW WAR BETTER THAN ANYONE ELSE on earth, that's no guarantee you'd be a good soldier. Knowledge alone doesn't get the job done. The same is true about marketing. Knowing about it is a good thing, but unless you maneuver your knowledge into action, it's pretty meaningless. It's knowledge plus action that's going to get you to your goals and beyond.

That's why we're writing this book. We've authored many valuable guerrilla marketing books that offer a wealth of secrets, strategies, tips, tactics, and tools—but this is the first one that shows you how to drive *momentum*. Notice how sparingly we've used italics throughout this book, yet we've chosen to italicize this one word. We want to demonstrate how important momentum is. We want you to fully embrace the meaning of momentum. It's crucial that you do. Because only then will you be ready to launch a marketing attack that is fully primed for success.

This field guide was created to teach you maneuvers to build powerful momentum. It will set you on a course of action designed to unleash your guerrilla expertise upon a market that needs you, while at the same time eliminating the competition.

In this field guide, we offer you 30 battlefield-tested maneuvers that will breathe vibrant life into your battle plan and stay with you the rest of your life. These maneuvers will help you clarify your mission, broaden your knowledge of what steps must be taken, and direct you to the specific action you must take that will lead to results.

These brief maneuvers will provide all the momentum you need to be a true guerrilla. You'll get the most out of these maneuvers if you complete them step by step, in the order they're presented, and within a short period of time. You must trust your instincts. This is not a game. This is real life. The orders in these pages will give you the knowledge you need to march into battle with confidence.

We know you can do it because others have done it before you, achieving high levels of success—both financially and emotionally. Completing these maneuvers will enable you to engage in marketing battles armed with competence and certainty. You'll no longer be a foot soldier. Instead, you'll be a guerrilla marketer, armed with everything it takes to make victory the norm for your life.

MAP OUT YOUR ATTACK

Before you set off for battle, you have got to know where you are going and what you expect to accomplish. An army doesn't march off without knowing where its enemy is located or without specific goals for what it needs to accomplish to ensure victory. It works the same way in business. You can't create momentum for your business if you charge off down the wrong road. So, first decide where you want to wind up, then create a roadmap that you know you can follow to your destination.

Your ultimate goal of running your own business is to create a profit. You may only want to work a few days a month and earn just enough to allow you to take nice vacations or buy a new car. Or you may be willing to work 24/7 if you can earn enough to retire comfortably in ten years. So, your first Maneuver is to spend some time considering your ultimate goals and what you need to earn to accomplish those goals.

Maneuver #1
DETERMINE YOUR BUSINESS GOALS

Express your business goals in terms of the amount of income (profit) you want each month and the number of days off you want each month. Do this for the first, third, and fifth years from today.

YEAR ONE

The amount of profit I want is $ _____ per month.

I want _____ days off per month.

YEAR THREE

The amount of profit I want is $ _____ per month.

I want _____ days off per month.

YEAR FIVE

The amount of profit I want is $ _____
per month.

I want _____ days off per month.

ASSESS YOUR ADVANTAGES

Now that you know where you want to go, you can use our battle plans to help you build the momentum you need to get there. But to put our battle strategy into action, you must first know why anyone would choose to do business with you rather than with your competitors. When you can answer that question, then you can determine and exploit your competitive advantage—something you'll utilize in all of your marketing.

Everybody touts benefits in their marketing, but guerrillas stress their unique benefits and play up the things they do better than anyone else. That's where you hang your marketing hat. That's your competitive advantage.

Many of today's products and services are so similar to each other that the only difference comes in how they are marketed. Businesses try to woo new customers with jingles, special effects, gimmicks, sales, and fancy production. These marketing devices are the final refuge of people with limited imaginations. Although there is little question that such techniques can help sales, a serious guerrilla knows other ways to market with far more potency.

And we repeat: your most important marketing tactic is making people understand your competitive advantages. If your widget doubles a company's profits, grows hair on bald heads, or attracts lifelong partners, you don't have to stoop to using advertising gimmicks. Just the truth will do very nicely, thank you. Jingles will just get in the way of clarity.

Perhaps you have so many competitive advantages, you don't know how to promote them all. Then, the only ones you should consider bringing to market are those that translate into instant profits for your company. A new method of dramatic fabrication will probably only bore your prospects, unless the benefits are as dazzling as the marketing spin and conveyance.

Perhaps you can't really see any marketable competitive advantages at your company. Realize that a savvy guerrilla discovers or creates them. The area most fertile for creating a new competitive advantage is service.

For example, there are gobs of automobile detailers in Marin County. All of them charge about the same price, do about the same job. So why did we pick P&H Class Details to detail our car? Because they make house calls. We didn't have to waste one second of precious time attending to the details of detailing. Instead, we made a phone call and P&H took over from there.

We were impressed by P&H's competitive advantage, though they didn't offer it when they started in business. But at some point, P&H surveyed the competitive scene, realized a detailing service could be a competitive advantage, created one, and advertised it. That's exactly why we're recommending that you zero in on an area that could be your competitive advantage.

See what your competitors are offering. Patronize them if you can, and keep an eagle eye open for areas in which you can surpass them, especially in service. Perhaps you can offer faster delivery, on-site service, gift wrapping, more frequent follow-up, maintenance for a period of time, installation, a longer guarantee, training, shipping—the possibilities are virtually endless.

A customer questionnaire will turn up many nifty areas upon which you may concentrate. Ask why people patronize the businesses they do. Ask what the ideal business would offer. Ask what they like best about your company. Pay close attention to the answers because some might be pointing directly at the competitive advantages you might want to offer.

Does it cost much to offer a competitive advantage? Nope. It takes brainpower, time, energy and imagination, but it is not a matter of money.

It may be that you already have a competitive advantage that is not yet marketed as such. Back in the 1930s, a copywriter went for a tour of the Lucky Strike cigarette factory. When he came across a large warm room filled with tobacco, he asked the person giving the tour what it was all about. "Oh, that's our toasting room," said the tour leader. "Do all cigarette companies have toasting rooms?" asked the canny copywriter. "Sure, they all do," was the answer.

But nobody else was marketing their toasting rooms. So, the writer suggested that Luckies say, "It's toasted!" right on the front of the package. The marketing director complied, and pretty soon the brand became America's number-one seller—all by emphasizing a detail held by all cigarette companies but not recognized as a marketing tool by the company's competition.

Such stories are legion. The important thing for you to do is to identify or create your own, then let it propel you to victory.

To begin to find your competitive advantage, make a list of the benefits only you offer. (You will find a place to do this at the end of this chapter.) Which of those are most important to your prospects? Once you have identified those competitive advantages, you've got a ticket to ride—all the way to the bank.

FIND PROBLEMS AND THEN SOLVE THEM

During your search, focus on problems that besiege your prospects. A well-known axiom of guerrilla marketing has always been that it is much simpler to sell the solution to a problem than it is to sell a positive benefit. For this reason, guerrillas position their companies as ace problem-solvers. They hone in on the problems confronting their prospects and then offer their products or services as solutions to those problems.

Everybody's got problems. Your job, as a right-thinking guerrilla, is to spot those problems. One of the ways to do this is through networking. Networking is not just a time to toot your own trombone, but to ask questions, listen carefully to the answers, and keep your marketing radar attuned to the presence of problems—particularly those being experienced by your potential clients. After learning about those problems, you can develop some solutions and then contact the prospect and offer your unique solutions.

You can also learn of problems that require solving at trade shows, professional association meetings, prospect questionnaires, and even sales calls. As you already know, people do not buy shampoo; they buy clean, great-looking hair. That is called selling the benefit. For example, some shampoo companies don't just state the obvious product benefit of cleaning hair; they also offer their shampoo as a solution to a known consumer problem, such as dry or damaged hair.

Right now, products and services that are enjoying success are those that help people quit smoking, lose weight, earn more money, improve health, grow hair, avoid foreclosure, eliminate wrinkles, and save time. Those are problem-solving products and services.

Your biggest job is to be sure your products and services do the same. Perhaps you'll have to undergo major repositioning to accomplish this. That's not a bad thing, if it improves your profits. Far more doors will be open to you if you can achieve it.

It's really not that difficult to position yourself or your business as a problem-solver. And once you do, you'll find that the task of marketing becomes a whole lot easier in a hurry. You need to examine your offerings in light of how they affect your prospects—not just provide a laundry list of your product's features. How many of your prospects care if the items you sell are state-of-the-art? But they will care a great deal if your product or service can reduce their overhead.

Prospects don't really care about your company; they care about their problems. If you can solve those problems, then prospects will become clients who want to buy what you are selling and who will care a great deal about your company.

Amazingly, even though this concept is so simple and so sensible, many companies are unaware of the importance of problem-solving. They're so wrapped up in the glories of their product or service that they are oblivious to how well it solves problems. So they tout features and neglect benefits. They try to sell the concept of how to "attain positive results" instead of "how to eliminate the negative results."

Keep the concept of problem-solving alive in your mind, and make it the centerpiece of your marketing, your sales presentations, and your advertising. Be sure your employees are tuned into the same wave-length. When everyone is focused on solving clients' problems, your business will take off, and we have a feeling that you're going to be one happy guerrilla.

---★---

Maneuver #2
LIST THE BENEFITS YOU OFFER

Now that you know how important it is to understand your competitive advantages, let's figure out what advantages your business has. Use this space (and the margins and clean paper if you need it) to list all the benefits of doing business with your company. Don't be shy. List every possible benefit you can think of no matter how minor it might seem.

The following are the benefits of doing business with my company:

_____

_____

_____

_____

_____

_____

_____

_____

_____

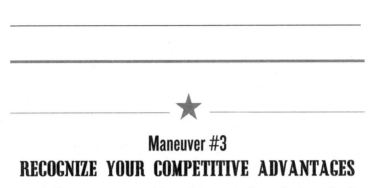

Maneuver #3
RECOGNIZE YOUR COMPETITIVE ADVANTAGES

Now, select your competitive advantages from the benefits list you just created.

My competitive advantages are:

_____

_____

_____

_____

_____

Maneuver #4
KNOW YOUR COMPETITORS

Your competitors may not know you, but the more you know about them, the better. Information is power, and you need all the power you can get. Learn about those competitors by buying from them and seeing how professional (or amateur) they are. Figure out their marketing plans. Call and ask challenging questions to see how they treat you. Do they follow up after purchases? Do they have referral plans? Are they givers or takers? All of these are important questions—and the list doesn't end there. The more thorough your answers, the easier it will be to beat those guys at their own games. Use the space below to list what you know about your most-feared competitor. Then create similar lists about your other competitors.

My biggest and best competitor is:

_____

This is what I know about that competitor:

_____

_____

_____

_____

_____

_____

_____

_____

_____

_____

_____

Maneuver #5
IDENTIFY YOUR TARGET MARKETS

Now that you know what competitive advantages your business has over your competition and you know what your competitors are offering their customers, let's think about what markets would be most interested in your advantages, so that you can target your marketing and advertising to them. The more target markets you have, the more profits you will earn. You may have one target market, but in all likelihood you have several.

Use geographical, demographic, and psychographic criteria to define your markets. Always prioritize the market that most resembles the makeup of your current customers. You might try listing a different target market for each competitive advantage you have identified above. Give this some thought and then jot down your answers here.

_____

_____

_____

_____

_____

_____

_____

_____

_____

_____

_____

_____

_____

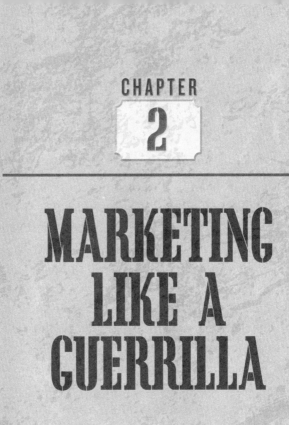

CHAPTER 2

MARKETING LIKE A GUERRILLA

⭐

MARKETING HAS CHANGED DRAMATICALLY SINCE THE first print ad was published. That ad was probably run in a local newspaper. More than likely, a farmer told the publisher that he had an extra cow and wanted to sell it. The publisher said, "Hey! I've got a good idea. Let me mention that cow for sale next time I publish my paper." The copy probably read: "Cow for sale. $50. Contact Farmer Tom Adams." The ad was run, the cow was sold, and marketing started.

It's not quite so simple these days. But two things remain the same. The first is that you need a good idea if you're going to do any marketing. Selling that cow was a pretty good idea back then. Today, you need to have a good idea of what you are selling and why and who would be interested in buying.

You also need a marketing strategy. Farmer Tom Adams' strategy was very simple: Sell one cow by having potential buyers come see him—and the cow. The benefit offered was a healthy cow at a fair price. The secondary benefit was that a local person was doing the selling. The target audience was other farmers in the community. The marketing weapon used was one ad in one newspaper. The niche the farmer occupied was that of a local farmer with an honest offer. The identity of the advertiser was straightforward and no-nonsense. And his marketing budget was most likely zero. Armed with that strategy, Farmer Tom sold his cow.

Today, several centuries after the first ad was published, you still need a good idea. And you still need a solid marketing strategy. Our world is much more complex than Farmer Tom's world was, so it may seem like you will also need a complex marketing strategy. But in reality, your strategy does not have to be complex. In fact, such a strategy needs only seven simple sentences. Regardless of the complexity of your offering, you must begin with a marketing strategy that's just as simple.

We're pretty sure you don't sell cows. But let's just suppose that you do sell adventure tours. And suppose the name of your company is Galactic Tours. Here's how you'd craft your strategy:

1. The first sentence tells the physical act your marketing should motivate.

   "THE PURPOSE OF GALACTIC TOURS MARKETING IS TO MOTIVATE PEOPLE TO CALL, WRITE, OR CLICK ON OUR WEBSITE REQUESTING A FREE VIDEO BROCHURE."

2. The second sentence spells out the prime benefit you offer.

   THE MAIN BENEFIT STRESSED WILL BE THE UNIQUE AND EXCITING DESTINATIONS THAT GALACTIC TOURS' CUSTOMERS CAN VISIT.

3. The third sentence states your target audience or audiences.

   OUR TARGET AUDIENCE SHOULD BE ADVENTUROUS MALES AND FEMALES, BOTH SINGLES AND COUPLES, 21 TO 34, WHO HAVE THE FINANCIAL RESOURCES TO AFFORD A GALACTIC TOUR.

4. The fourth sentence states what marketing weapons you plan to use.

   WE WILL REACH OUR TARGET AUDIENCE BY PLACING ADS IN HIGH-END MAGAZINES, CREATING A WEBSITE AND FACEBOOK PAGE, AND PLACING ADS ON THE OUTDOOR TV NETWORK.

5. In your fifth sentence, you define your niche or what you stand for: economy, service, quality, price, uniqueness, anything.

   OUR NICHE IS CONVENIENCE AT AN AFFORDABLE PRICE PROVIDED BY VERY WELL-TRAINED GUIDES.

6. The sixth sentence states the personality of your company.

   THE PERSONALITY OF GALACTIC TOURS WILL REFLECT INNOVATION, EXCITEMENT, AND A WARM, CARING ATTITUDE TOWARD ALL CUSTOMERS.

7. The seventh sentence states your marketing budget, expressed as a percentage of your projected gross sales.

   "GALACTIC TOURS WILL INVEST 10% OF GROSS REVENUES IN MARKETING."

Is that all there is to it?

Yep. That's all. Procter and Gamble—a company so successful that 97 percent of homes in America have at least one of their products—uses the same type of simple strategy for all its brands. And most of those brands are either the number-one or number-two sellers in their categories. True, P&G may have umpteen pages of documentation and details as well, but they begin with a very simple and clear strategy, just like the one you just read.

"Marketing strategy" is merely a fancy phrase that means *determining what you want and how you'll get it.* If you don't have one, you really have no business marketing in the first place. And it sure won't cost you much to get one.

KEEP YOUR STRATEGY BRIEF

A brief guerrilla marketing strategy forces you to focus upon the people targeted by your marketing. Always start with the people and then work backward to the offering. Such a strategy zeros in on the results you want to achieve, the way you plan to obtain those results, and the specific action you want your target audience to take. It provides you with a guide for judging all of your marketing efforts for the next 10 or 20 years.

The strategy must be expressed in writing, and it should not contain headlines, theme lines, or copy. The strategy is totally devoid of specific marketing copy because it must be solid, yet flexible. Specific words and phrases pin you down. A guerrilla strategy should be developed as your guide, not as your master.

Just like a Procter and Gamble strategy, yours should be deceptively simple when you first read it, but writing it will not be that easy. After you've written all seven steps, read it a couple of times, then put it away for 24 hours. It's just too important to be accepted—or rejected—hastily. Look at your strategy from a fresh perspective on a different day. See if you still love it and believe in it.

Always remember that your strategy is supposed to generate handsome returns on your marketing investment for years to come. All future ads, commercials, tweets, signs, websites, Facebook postings, brochures, and many business decisions will be measured against it.

KEEP YOUR STRATEGY FOCUSED

When is the best time to change that strategy? The first time you see it—before you've invested any money in it. After you've finalized it, don't change it again for at least six months; then do a review and see if you need to tweak your strategy. If you have it right, you may not need to make any changes for several years.

Your approved strategy should be pinned up on bulletin boards and emblazoned in the minds of everyone who creates marketing for you. Keep the strategy handy in a drawer, on your desktop, or in an accessible file so that you can reach for it the moment anyone presents even a tiny opportunity for marketing to you . . . or when you have a killer idea yourself. Best, of course, is to memorize it.

What if you absolutely love the marketing, but it does not fulfill the strategy? Toss it away this very moment. Suppose you hate the marketing, but it does fulfill the strategy? Then give it a second thought. At least it's 50 percent of the way home.

Guerrillas know that the single most important element of superb marketing is commitment to a focused plan. Do you think commitment is easy to maintain after an ad has run 19 times and nobody is buying? It's not easy. But marketing guerrillas have the coolness to hang in there because they know how to get into a prospect's unconsciousness, where most purchase decisions are made. They know it takes repetition. This knowledge fuels their commitment. Anyhow, they never thought it was going to be easy.

The mantra goes that real estate is all about location, location, location. Marketing is frequency, frequency, frequency. That's what we mean by commitment.

Now that you know what we mean by marketing strategy, it's time for you to create one for yourself. Use the momentum-building Maneuvers below to get started.

Maneuver #6
WRITE YOUR SEVEN-SENTENCE GUERRILLA MARKETING STRATEGY

Ask yourself these questions so that you can create your seven-sentence marketing strategy.

1. What physical act do I want people to take after being exposed to my marketing (click here, call a phone number, complete this coupon, or look for my product next time they're at the store)? _____

_____

_____

_____

2. What prime benefit do I offer? What competitive advantage do I want to stress? _____

_____

_____

_____

_____

3. Who is my target audience? _____

_____

_____

_____

_____

4. What marketing weapons will I use? (You can read the
guerrilla marketing and social media weapons listed in
Appendix A and Appendix B to get ideas.) _____

_____

_____

_____

_____

5. What will my market niche be? _____

_____

_____

_____

_____

6. What identity do I want my business to have? _____

_____

_____

_____

7. My marketing budget will be _____% of our projected gross sales.

★

Maneuver #7
CREATE YOUR ELEVATOR PITCH

Now that you have a marketing strategy, it's time to start creating marketing messages. The first message you should work on is your "elevator pitch." Crafting an elevator pitch is an excellent way to create momentum for yourself. After you have honed this maneuver, you can more easily determine what you want to say on your website, in your mailings, and in other advertising or marketing material.

Pretend you're in an elevator with your perfect target customer. You have 30 seconds to tell that person what you do or sell and get them interested in your business. At the end of the 30 seconds, they should be left wanting to know more, instead of being glad to get away from you. Write your elevator pitch, include your all-important competitive advantage, then practice it till you know it backward and forward but it doesn't sound memorized, and you can deliver it in 30 seconds. You need to be able to clearly articulate the most important parts about your business to someone who doesn't even know you—in 30 seconds.

My elevator pitch is:

_____

_____

_____

_____

_____

_____

_____

_____

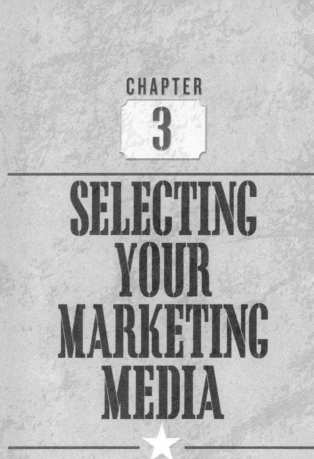

CHAPTER

3

SELECTING YOUR MARKETING MEDIA

★

O K, SO YOU'VE GOT A GOOD HANDLE ON YOUR MARKETING strategy. You have seven sentences that will remind you of the identity and niche of your business, what it offers, and what you want your marketing to accomplish. You can summarize what your business does or offers in 30 seconds or less.

As you developed your marketing strategy and your elevator pitch, you spent some time thinking about your target audience—those people who ought to own what you're selling but, for some reason, don't as of yet. Now you've got to determine the most effective way of reaching them and speaking to them.

We love the speed, convenience, and economy of email. But that's not the only way to get people off the fence and onto your customer list. Sometimes, you can do that with newspapers. Other times, you need magazines—consumer or business. On other occasions, you'll need radio or TV. Then there are the reliable standbys of brochures and billboards.

But let's not forget the fastest-growing, most immediate methods of grabbing customers' attention today: mobile marketing through smartphones and tablets and banner ads or links on the omnipotent internet. Here's a major tip: *Guerrillas realize that you will almost certainly need a combination of media to get results.*

Whether it's email, direct mail, postcard decks, telemarketing, newsletters, catalogues, infomercials, home shopping shows, online marketing, canvassing, trade shows, or networking functions, *almost all marketing works much better when it is combined with other marketing efforts.* In a heated battle, you never have to choose between using a gun or a bomb. You must use both or you're going to lose that battle.

So don't begin to market the split-second after you complete writing your battle plan (marketing strategy). First, decide which of the marketing weapons you will employ, so you can load your marketing guns with live ammo instead of blanks. Marketing without a plan makes a lot of noise, but doesn't generate profits—or hurt enemies.

When selecting the media that will hit your target audience right where they live—or work—consider the environment in which your marketing will appear. Pick the media that best reaches your audience, and adapt your marketing messages to fit the moods of your readers, listeners, viewers, or visitors. It's easier than ever to create highly specialized messages with the highly specialized media now available.

KNOW THE POWER OF YOUR WEAPON

You can't lob artillery shells with a rifle; your ammunition must match your weapon. In the same way, what works in one medium may not work in another. Guerrillas learn the powers of each medium and then tap those strengths to use the medium to its greatest advantages. They realize that these days the media appears both online and offline. Here's what they know about the media power of both.

★ *The power of newspapers and news-oriented websites and blogs is news.* In these media, marketing that is newsy gets noticed. People now get news from many different sources, including newspapers, magazines, cable news stations, blogs, newsletters, Facebook postings, tweets, RSS feeds, and internet radio. Use these sources to target an audience that is well-informed and appreciates a fact-filled, straightforward approach.

★ *The power of magazines is credibility.* Readers unconsciously attach to the advertiser the same credibility that they associate with the magazine. Match your message to the tone and style of the magazine if you want the readers to notice it.

★ *The power of radio is intimacy.* Usually radio is consumed in a one-on-one situation allowing for an intimate connection between listener and marketer. Radio marketing messages must make a connection on that same intimate level.

★ *The power of direct mail is urgency.* Time-dated offers coax the recipient into acting quickly if they think the opportunity will expire soon.

★ *The power of telemarketing is rapport.* Few media allow you to establish contact in a give-and-take situation as adroitly as the telephone.

★ *The power of brochures is the ability to provide details.* Few media allow you the time and space to expand on your benefits as much as a brochure.

★ *The power of classified ads is information.* Nobody in their right mind actually reads the classified ads, except for those in a quest for data.

★ *The power of the Yellow Pages is even more information.* Here, prospects get a line on the entire competitive situation and then compare. Today, people expect search engines to do the work of the Yellow Pages. But we'd advise you to utilize both, depending on your exact competitive situation.

★ *The power of TV is the ability to demonstrate.* No other media lets you show your product or service in use along with the benefits it offers. The internet is great and still growing, but TV is still the undisputed heavyweight champ of marketing.

★ *The power of the internet is interactivity.* You can flag viewers' attention, inform them, answer their questions, direct them to your site, and take their orders. You can initiate a dialogue with customers on their schedule and have them even engage with each other—a major advantage.

★ *The power of signs is an impulse reaction.* Signs motivate people to buy when they are in a buying mood and in a buying arena. Signs either trigger an impulse, remind people of your other marketing, or both.

★ *The power of fliers is economy.* They can be created, produced, and distributed for very little and can sometimes bring about instant results.

★ *The power of billboards is to remind.* They rarely do the whole selling job, but they're great at jostling people's memories about your business.

Guerrillas are aware of the specific powers of each medium and design their marketing as to capitalize upon them. Adjusting the message to the medium is an art and a necessity. All media were not created equal. Guerrillas are quick to take advantage of these inequalities so they can increase the effectiveness of each weapon they use.

NOT AN ARMY OF ONE

Always keep in mind that your media messages work better if they're supported by messages in other media. You're not really promoting unless you're *cross*-promoting. Mention your website in your TV commercial. Mention your radio ad in your direct mail. Refer to your email in your telemarketing. Your trade show booth will be far more valuable to you if you promote it in trade magazines and place fliers in hotels near the trade show. Guerrillas try to market their marketing.

Your prospects pay attention to a lot of media, and different personalities respond to one message better than another. So you can't depend on a mere one medium to motivate a purchase. You're got to introduce a notion, remind people of it, say it again, then repeat it in different words somewhere else. How do guerrilla marketers grab mindshare? They get it when they combine several media. They say in their ads, "Call, write, text, or email for our free brochure."

They say in their Yellow Pages ad, "Get even more details at our website." They enclose a copy of their magazine ad in their mailing. They blow up a copy of a newspaper ad to use as a sign. Their email makes it easy to click to their website. Their website features their print ads.

Guerrillas are quick to mention their use of one medium while using another because they realize that people equate broad-scale marketing with quality and success. They know that people trust names they've heard of much more than strange and new names, and guerrillas are realistic enough to know that people miss most marketing messages—often intentionally. The remote control not only allows a TV watcher to stay on the couch, but also allows them to eliminate marketing messages.

No matter how glorious their newspaper campaign may be, guerrillas realize that not all of their prospects read the paper so they've got to get to these people in another way. This is especially true now that fewer people read newspapers. The same concept holds true online. No matter how dazzling your website, it's like a grain of sand in a desert; no one will see it unless you promote it wisely to an unknowing and indifferent public.

Cross-promoting through several types of media is another way to accomplish the all-important task of repetition. One way to repeat yourself and implant your message is to say it over and over again. Another way is to say it in several different places. Guerrillas try to do both. Nothing is left to chance.

If you have ever opened an email with an offer from a company you've never heard of and another with the same offer, which was promoted "As advertised on TV," you'd probably opt for the second because of that added smidgen of credibility. Credibility creates confidence, and confidence creates sales.

So, how do you know what media to use and how to create the right message for that media? You ask your customers. And how do you keep track of which media you have used/ are using/will use to promote your business? You can also ask other businesses about the possibility of banding together to market your products, a type of "Fusion Marketing." These next Maneuvers can help you put all these ideas to use.

Maneuver #8
ASK YOUR CUSTOMERS

Knowledge is power. The more you know about your customers and prospects, the more effectively you can reach them and better serve their needs. So, ask them. Use surveys to learn all about them. You can ask them questions when they buy something in your store or on your website or use Survey Monkey (surveymonkey.com) to create and send a survey through email or online. Check the resources on the SurveyMonkey site to figure out how to do this.

Remember, if you are allowing respondents to remain anonymous, they are more likely to answer lots of important personal questions, such as income and lifestyle, and favorite TV shows, social media sites, sports teams, and hobbies. Ask them which TV shows they watch, which radio stations they listen to, what magazines and newspapers they read, and which internet sites they visit regularly. Be sure to ask what people like most about your company and where they'd expect you to advertise or do your marketing.

List questions you want your customers to answer:

1. _____

2. _____

3. _____

4. _____

5. _____

6. _____

7. _____

8. _____

9. _____

10. _____

Maneuver #9
FIND FUSION MARKETING PARTNERS

Fusion marketing lets you spread your marketing wings while reducing your marketing costs. Also known as tie-ins, fusion marketing is coming into its own now more than ever. Form an alliance with other companies who will help you market your company while you help market theirs. Many companies have 20 or more fusion marketing arrangements; however, you should start by considering only five companies with whom you could establish a collaborative marketing arrangement. Remember: Your fusion marketing partners must share both your target markets and your high standards of excellence.

My prospective fusion marketing partners are:

1. _____

2. _____

3. _____

4. _____

5. _____

★

Maneuver #10
PLAN YOUR GUERRILLA MARKETING CALENDAR

Your Guerrilla Marketing calendar enables you to decide which media to use and when. With this calendar, you can spread your messages out to various media and make sure that you are using every available weapon to reach your target audience. It will allow you to project three years into the future and will only get more valuable as those years pass because you'll be able to track your progress and see what marketing messages are most successful. Many businesses report that they need three years to create a calendar in order to map out slam-dunk successes for each month.

Start by creating your calendar for the first year. The first column, "Month," needs no explanation. (Hint: There are 12 of them.) Your "Message" is the prime idea you wish to communicate that month. Your "Weapons" are—we hope—your website, blended with a host of other media. The "Cost" is what it really and truly costs you. And the "Grade" is your instinctive reaction to what kind of month you had: A, B, C, D, or F. Be not only a professor here, but also a tough grader.

Next year, you'll take the winners from the first year, add more marketing weapons, and keep going. You'll repeat this again at the start of your third marketing year—and that's when you should be getting your 4.0 marketing grade point average. That, guerrillas tell us, is like entering heaven without the inconvenience of dying.

At first, just complete your calendar for the next 12 months only:

YEAR ONE

MONTH	MESSAGE	WEAPON	COST	GRADE
January				
February				
March				
April				
May				
June				
July				
August				
September				
October				
November				
December				

YEAR TWO

MONTH	MESSAGE	WEAPON	COST	GRADE
January				
February				
March				
April				
May				
June				
July				
August				
September				
October				
November				
December				

YEAR THREE

MONTH	MESSAGE	WEAPON	COST	GRADE
January				
February				
March				
April				
May				
June				
July				
August				
September				
October				
November				
December				

PUTTING YOUR CREDIBILITY ON STEROIDS

E VERY GUERRILLA KNOWS THAT THE NUMBER-ONE FACTOR influencing purchase decisions is confidence. Customers must be confident they will get a good deal if they buy from you. And the road to customer confidence is paved with credibility—your credibility. Even guerrilla marketing can't pave that road if it is full of potholes. Here's where you learn to build a solid foundation of credibility and reliability.

Having the lowest price won't help you much if your prospect doesn't trust you in the first place. Offering the widest selection and the most convenience won't aid your cause if your prospect thinks you're a crook.

You've got to face up to the glaring reality that prospects won't call your toll-free number, access your website, mail your coupon, come into your store, visit your trade show booth, talk to your sales rep, talk to you on the phone, visit your Facebook page, tweet you, or even accept your generous freebie if they aren't confident in your company.

In order to earn that confidence—no stroll in the park, as you've most likely learned—you must arm yourself with guerrilla marketing weapons and use them *properly*. We emphasize "properly" because even a smart bomb isn't a valuable weapon if it lands on your foot.

PAY ATTENTION TO META-MESSAGES

Guerrillas don't think putting camouflage over problems will bring credibility. Instead, they know you have to earn your credibility by your achievements and your actions. They know that all their marketing materials carry a *meta-message*—an unstated, yet powerful communiqué to a prospect. A large, handsome ad in a respected publication carries a much more potent meta-message than a small, crude-looking ad in a free

Let's use Deuce Cleaners as an example. If they create a superbly written direct-mail letter yet send it out on inexpensive stationery, the meta-message is going to be quite different from that of their competitor, Ace Cleaners. Ace's direct-mail letter carries a similar message, but it was printed on upscale stationery that looks and feels exquisite and features a clear and elegant typeface and a signature that was hand-signed using blue ink and a fountain pen.

Although paper stock and signatures are not as important as they were before the "Digital Age," they still carry a strong meta-message, as does a real stamp. The typeface of any message speaks volumes, and the printed—or handwritten—signature lends an eloquent touch. These may seem like minor details; they are tiny, but nuclear-powered.

Not surprisingly, the Deuce Cleaners letter, even though worded exactly like the Ace Cleaners letter, will not draw as healthy a response because of its weak meta-message. *A powerful meta-message inspires confidence.*

newspaper. Always keep in mind that meta-messages have just as much impact as your stated messages in your marketing materials.

Entire marketing plans fall by the wayside because inattention to details undermines the prospect's confidence in your ability to conduct your business—even if you had previously earned that confidence elsewhere. Any hint of amateurism in your marketing indicates to your prospects that amateurism may exist elsewhere in your company. An amateurish logo or meme makes a statement to your partners and customers that you don't know what you're doing. A busy website that's tough to navigate or contains irritating graphics spells disaster.

Absolutely everything you do that is visible to your customers influences your credibility. The influence will be positive or negative, depending upon your taste, intelligence, sensitivity, and awareness of this power.

Be aware of this the moment you launch your business. Start the quest with the name of your company, your logo, your theme line, location, stationery, business card, package, brochure, business forms, interior decor, website, fusion marketing partners, and even the attire worn by you and your employees. Convey your credibility to the largest number of people with your marketing, as all of those factors can play an important part in your success.

You need to be sure you communicate the right message in all areas of your business, not just your marketing materials. Pay attention to the look and feel of your building and office, the appearance and manner of the people you employ, the technology you use, how you engage people with follow-ups, the testimonials you display, the appearance of your trade show booth, and the quality of your signs.

Some companies pay no attention to how their phones are answered—if they are even answered at all. Recently, we were prepared to make an expensive purchase from a store by telephone, but we changed our minds simply because customer service put us on hold for too long. Are we too impatient? Maybe—but somebody else now has our deposit check, and you can bet there are a lot more customers out there like us.

SHOWCASE YOUR EXPERTISE

You gain credibility with your advertisements, listings in directories, columns and articles you write, and talks you give. You gain even more credibility when you publicly support a noble cause, such as the environment. These little things add up to something called your *reputation*.

You can also earn credibility by taking actions outside of your business. Give a seminar. Volunteer your skills for a community organization. The idea is for you to establish your expertise, authority, integrity, conscientiousness, and professionalism—all affect your credibility. The more you have, the better your marketing will work. The better your marketing works, the more credibility you'll have. It's a merry-go-round ride you're going to love.

When your company gets mentioned in the newspaper, make reprints of the article and frame them for your store counter and shop window. Include them on your website (with links) and in your brochures, newsletters, and ads. Cost? A bit of time. Result? A lot of credibility.

TAKE A SHORTCUT

Would you like a shortcut to achieving credibility? Run a full-page ad in a regional edition of a national magazine. The ad by itself won't net much credibility, but the reprints you display, mail, incorporate into other marketing, and proudly disseminate will. They'll all proclaim: "As advertised in *Time* magazine."

All the credibility of that magazine—along with its millions of readers—suddenly become attached to you. We're not talking zillions of dollars here—just a one-time expense of a few thousand. It's a small price to pay for credibility. It's even smaller if you advertise in a business magazine or trade journal. If you're looking for the best possible price on the ad, type in "remnant space" on the magazine's website and ask for the media kit.

When magazines are printed, they are four-page units all connected like a piece of paper folded in half. Often, editorial material or advertising appears on three of the pages, but sometimes that fourth page has nothing on it. Magazines can't make money with blank pages, so they sell that remnant space to small advertisers who get the credibility for a fraction of the usual investment.

As I warned readers in the original *Guerrilla Marketing* book, media rate cards are like Harry Potter books—fun to read but based on fantasy. In truth, media costs are dependent upon plain and simple negotiation and not what they say in the rate card.

We keep reminding you that magazines give you tons of credibility. We do this because we know your prospects can always choose to do business with you or with your competitors. Who do you suppose they choose—the company with impressive credibility or the one with zero credibility?

Because credibility affects profitability, you need to know how to get it without investing too much money. You do that by becoming the expert. The next Maneuvers will show you how to do that.

★

Maneuver #11
BECOME THE EXPERT

Credibility paves your path to sales and profits. You earn credibility by becoming a known expert on your subject. How can you do that? Try writing articles, columns, a blog, or a book; publishing that book; giving lectures; creating a powerful e-newsletter. It's important that you offer real information of worth and value in these venues without charging and without selling products, but mention your company name and website. Use the prompts below to help locate ways you can become the expert.

I will establish credibility and become an acknowledged expert by:

_____

_____

_____

_____

_____

_____

_____

_____

_____

_____

Maneuver #12
GIVE TALKS

You now realize that your target market prefers doing with business with acknowledged experts. One of the all-time best ways to prove your expertise and bond with your prospects and customers is to give free talks to local and regional organizations. This technique can be invaluable because you'll give the audience real information they can use to improve their lives and their businesses. Nothing builds relationships with your prospects more than them seeing you live and in person. Remember, the aim of these talks is to tell, never to sell. Don't worry, if you impress them with your expertise, people will remember you and will do business with you. In fact, the less selling you do in your talks, the more memorable you will be.

N ot comfortable speaking? Solvable problem. Join a local Toastmaster club, where you can practice giving speeches and refine both your content and delivery. There are clubs all over the world. Visit www. toastmasters.org to find a club near you. The benefits are enormous and the cost very minimal for you to be a star.

I will approach these organizations to arrange speaking engagements:

_____

_____

_____

_____

_____

_____

Maneuver #13
AUTHOR A BOOK

Published books—whether print, e-book, or both—provide an enormous amount of credibility. While it's great to find a major publisher who can distribute your book, self-publishing can also be a viable way to establish your authority. It's also possible for a self-published print or e-book to be acquired by a major publisher at a later date, if it's well done and it has market viability.

The book you write becomes your calling card. It can lead to speaking invitations, become the foundation for workshops and seminars, attract business, and establish you as the authority. After all, you wrote the book. Who knows better than you?

Of course, writing a book is not an easy task. You've got to do the research, organize your thinking, then put it all down clearly. If you know your topic and enjoy writing, being an author is a privilege. But if you know your topic and don't enjoy writing, it can be a painful task; in this case you might want to consider a collaborator or hiring a ghostwriter.

Are you an expert in your field? That gives you a running start as an author. Just think: There is no better business card than a book you've written and published.

I would like to write books on these topics:

_____

_____

_____

_____

_____

_____

_____

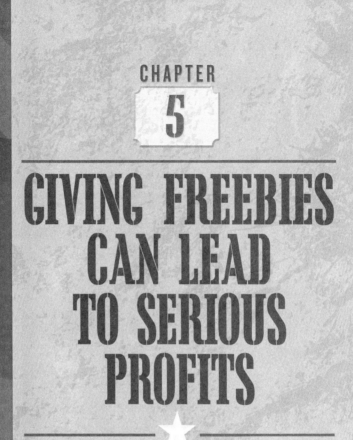

GIVING FREEBIES CAN LEAD TO SERIOUS PROFITS

★

THESE DAYS, THERE SEEM TO BE TWO KINDS OF BUSINESSES: givers and takers. Giver businesses are quick to give freebies to customers and prospects. The freebies most often come in the form of information. The right information is worth more than a gift and often far more than money.

We've always known guerrilla marketers were blessed with infinite patience and fertile imaginations. We've written in awe of their acute sensitivity and their admirable ego strength. We've raved about their aggressiveness in marketing and their penchant for constant learning. Now we've added a new personality trait to our list of characteristics possessed by successful guerrillas: generosity. They are generous souls who seem to gain joy by giving things away, by taking their customers and prospects beyond satisfaction and into true bliss. They learn what people want and need and then give to them for free.

The results: delighted prospects who become customers; delighted customers who become repeat customers; and delighted repeat customers who give referrals. Those are huge payoffs.

What kind of things do guerrilla marketers give away for free? Let's start with a list of ten, and your mind will be primed to dream up ten more.

1. They give gift certificates to their own businesses, whether the certificates are for products or services.
2. They give printed brochures to anybody who requests one.
3 They give electronic brochures—email, as well as audio and video downloads—to people who ask for them.
4. They give money to worthy causes and let their prospects and customers know that they support a noble

cause, enabling these people to support the same endeavor.

5. They give free consultations and never make them seem like sales presentations.

6. They give free seminars and clinics because they realize that if their information is worthwhile, it will attract the right kind of people.

7. They give free demonstrations to prove without words the worth of their offerings.

8. They give tours of their facilities or of work they've accomplished elsewhere, again transcending any standard marketing tools they might employ.

9. They give free samples because they know that such generosity is the equivalent of purchasing a new customer at a very low price.

10. They give invaluable information on their website, realizing that such data will bring their customers and prospects back for more, thereby intensifying their relationships.

In addition to these ten, guerrillas are highly creative dreaming up what they might give for free. Of course, many advertising specialties, such as calendars and scratchpads, mouse pads, and ballpoint pens are emblazoned with their names and theme lines, but they seem to exercise extra creativity as well.

★

Case in point: As an apartment building was being built, the owners put up signs proudly proclaiming that you get "Free Auto Grooming" when you sign a lease. Soon, the building's occupancy rate was 100 percent.

The salary for the guy who washes tenants' cars once a week was easily covered by the difference between 100 percent occupancy and 71 percent occupancy, the usual occupancy rate in that neighborhood.

That means your task is clear: Think of what might attract prospects and make customers happy. Be creative. Be generous. Then, be prepared for a reputation embracing generosity, customer service, and sincere caring.

WHAT CAN YOU GIVE AWAY?

Today's customers are attracted to giver companies and repelled by taker companies. What kind of company is yours?

When the economy declines, your business will probably slide with it. This is frightening, but on the good side, an economic downturn gives you the time to think freely. Spend some of that extra time considering what you can give your prospects for free. If you offer your product or service free for a limited time, you enable your prospects to feel like your customers and understand all of the advantages of doing business with you. You'll have a great opportunity to prove your company's superiority and they'll be far more likely to actually make the purchase.

You're in business because you offer a product or service that delivers desirable benefits. You're in business because you're better than many of your competitors. You're in business because you want to earn hefty and consistent profits.

As a guerrilla, you surpass customer satisfaction and allow those who patronize your business to experience customer bliss. They can tell how conscientious you are by means of your follow-up and the way you pay attention to details in their life and business.

There are many ways to offer freebies. You can offer gift certificates, coupons, brochures, free consultations, free demos, free seminars, free tours, and a wealth of free information on your website. HotMail attracted more than 50 million customers for its free email service. Now that service is supported by advertising. By ending each free email from the sender with a free email offer for the recipient, HotMail demonstrated highly creative and effective guerrilla marketing tactics.

It's true that some people sign up for freebies and then you'll never hear from them again. But many customers will become so impressed by your quality, service, caring, and dedication that they'll end up making the purchase you want them to make. Many will become lifelong customers, making you forget those freeloaders entirely.

We realize that it may not be possible for every company to give away what it normally sells. But if you can afford it, try giving away your centerpiece product or service for a limited time period. Test out this process once on a limited time period for a select number of customers—such as the first 100. Then you can gauge results and see if it's worth expanding the effort.

Maneuver #14
LEARN WHAT YOU CAN GIVE FOR FREE

Generosity is one of the hallmarks of guerrilla marketing. People are attracted to giver companies. So, think about what information or other valuable product or services can you give for free? Consider offering free consultations, demonstrations, samples, seminars, estimates, appraisals, delivery, installation, training, or mentoring. The more generous you are, the more profits you'll reap.

I can give away these things for free:

_____

_____

_____

_____

_____

_____

_____

_____

_____

_____

_____

★

Maneuver #15
BUILD CONSENT WITH SOFT STEPS

Of course you remember that guerrilla marketing is all about creating and maintaining relationships. How do you build a relationship? By creating a series of soft steps, such as

5 / Giving Freebies Can Lead to Serious Profits

free brochures, consultations, demonstrations, tours, samples, videos, audiotapes, booklets, estimates, seminars, newsletters, parties, special events, appraisals, and, of course, a website. You can build trust and rapport to gain consent from a prospect to take more soft steps, which eventually makes the customer's hard step of buying much easier. Then you maintain the relationship by providing many more after-sale soft steps that encourage your customers to remain loyal and make repeat purchases.

I will take these soft steps to build relationships with my customers:

1. _____

2. _____

3. _____

4. _____

5. _____

6. _____

7. _____

8. _____

9. _____

10. _____

11. _____

12. _____

13. _____

14. _____

15. _____

16. _____

17. _____

18. _____

19. _____

20. _____

CHAPTER

6

DISCOVERING MEMES—

THE NEWEST SECRET IN MARKETING

★

WE'VE WRITTEN ABOUT MEMES IN MOST OF OUR BOOKS since the close of the 20th century. We're going to write about them again because we want you to become the proud and profitable owner of your own meme. And we want it to be a good one.

A prehistoric man, Uba, spent all day in the rain trying to catch a fish because his family was very hungry and in dire need of food. Try as he might, he was unable to grab a fish from the stream even though he occasionally got his hands on one. Frustrated and weak from hunger, he just couldn't grab any fish firmly enough because each time it would slither from his hands and return to the stream. Worse yet, the light rain turned to heavy rain, and Uba was forced to seek shelter in a nearby cave.

Entering the cave, as his eyes adjusted to the darkness, he noticed a series of paintings. One depicted a deer. Another represented a godlike figure. But it was the third that captured his attention.

There on the cave wall was a simple drawing—a figure of a man holding a long stick. At the end of the stick, a fish was impaled. Suddenly, Uba got the idea and left the cave. Within an hour, he returned to his family carrying five fish at the end of a sharpened stick.

Uba's family was saved by a meme: a self-explanatory symbol that uses words, action, sounds, or in this case, pictures, to communicate an entire idea. Uba may have discovered the first meme in history.

Since Uba's time, there have been many more memes. In fact, as much as you used to see the word "internet," during the '90s, that's about as many times as you'll see the word "memes" in the future.

6 / Discovering Memes—The Newest Secret in Marketing

Memes in advertising are a whole new idea, though they have existed long before the concept was defined as such. The word *meme*, officially coined in 1976 by Oxford biologist Richard Dawkins in his book, *The Selfish Gene*, has been the architect of human behavior since the beginning of time. The wheel was a major improvement in transportation and conveyance; yet it was also a meme because it was a self-explanatory symbol representing a complete idea.

You should know three things about a meme:

1. It's the lowest common denominator of an idea, a basic unit of communication.
2. It has the ability to alter human behavior.
3. It is energized with emotion.

In guerrilla advertising, a meme's purpose is instantly communi-cating how your product or service improves lives, so that you can motivate customers to buy more, which will bring more profit for you. It can do this with words (Lean Cuisine), pictures (the Marlboro cowboy), sounds (from the valley of the Jolly "ho ho ho" Green Giant), actions (Clydesdales pulling Budweiser wagon), or imagery (Burger King's flame-broiled image). To put you even more on our wavelength, consider these other memes we have learned to know and possibly even love:

★ Healthy Choice
★ Be Direct—Dell
★ Intel Inside

★ Got Milk?
★ Capitalist Tool—Forbes
★ Panasonic—Just Slightly Ahead of Our Time
★ Where Do You Want to Go Today?
★ America Online
★ Drivers Wanted—VW
★ I'm Going to Disneyland!
★ UPS—Moving at the Speed of Business
★ M&Ms Melt In Your Mouth, Not In Your Hands
★ Slimfast
★ Weight Watchers
★ NBC—Must-See TV
★ A Diamond Is Forever
★ Toys R Us
★ Staples—Yeah, We've Got That
★ Footjoy
★ V for Victory
★ Gatorade Poured on Winning Coach
★ Things Go Better with Coke
★ 7-Up—The Uncola
★ I Want My MTV!
★ The Mall of America
★ Snap, Crackle, and Pop

For guerrillas, a meme is a concept that has been so simplified that anybody can understand it instantly and

Try to imagine a motorist speeding down a highway, just entering a curve. All of a sudden, a billboard comes into view. It shows a mutilated child, an ambulance, paramedics, flashing lights, weeping parents, and a grim police officer. The billboard copy reads: Speed kills.

The combined effect of the photo and two-word copy constitutes a meme that instantly, effortlessly, and lucidly transmits an entire complex message into a human mind in a single involuntary glance. If you saw it while driving, there is little doubt that you would cut your speed without even thinking about it.

easily. Within two seconds a good meme must convey who you are and why someone should buy from you instead of a competitor and trigger an emotional response that generates a desire. A meme is an idea or concept that has been refined, distilled, stripped downs to its bare essentials, then super-simplified in such a way that anybody can grasp its meaning instantly and effortlessly.

As you can see from the above example, memes have an enormous impact on our lives. They invade our minds without our knowledge or our permission and initiate a chain reaction. Memes create an involuntary shift in perception, which in turn creates a shift in attitude and then behavior; this is the ultimate goal of all marketing.

With so much marketing—both online and offline—assailing our senses, it's more important than ever to create a meme for your company. We didn't say it would be easy, but it is mandatory if you're going to stand out in an ever-competitive crowd—one that relishes its time more than ever. Don't be like Uba and wait until you're all wet and hungry.

★

Maneuver #16
CREATE A MEME

A meme is a visual or graphic representation that instantly communicates an entire idea. Memes can be verbal, such as "click here," or action, such as spraying champagne after winning a race. To create a meme, think of the prime benefits that you offer, then come up with a visual or brief verbal way of calling attention to them that instantly communicates what your company is all about—even to people who have never heard of what you do. (See Appendix C for **The Top Ten Marketing Memes**.)

My meme ideas include:

_____

CHAPTER 7

LEARNING TO BE A CREATIVE GUERRILLA

⭐

THE FIRST STEP IN BEING CREATIVE IS GAINING KNOWLEDGE. Just by completing the previous 16 battle plan Maneuvers, you've already proven that you have enough knowledge to spread your creative wings. You are now ready to become a guerrilla copywriter.

Guerrilla copywriting isn't about you, your product, your service, or your company. It's about your customer—or, more specifically, it's about telling your customers how what you offer would make their lives better. Once your customers know you can make life better, some of them will, at the very least, want to find out more about you and what you offer. Others may want to buy something from you right away. In either case—and everywhere in between—creating compelling copy about how you will make your customer's life better creates a relationship money cannot buy.

To discover your value proposition to the customer, you need to start with a benefits list. In fact, all guerrilla copy both starts and ends with a benefits list.

Here's how to write your list: Call a meeting. Invite your key personnel and at least one customer. Your customers are tuned into benefits that you may not even consider benefits. Listen ... and write. You are paying close attention to needs and wants, which can be converted into benefits.

With your benefits list and your competitive advantage available, you now have the bricks and mortar of all your copy, whether it is to be used on a website, in a tweet, on a blog post, in a radio ad, in a national magazine, or in a flier at a local flea market. With your benefits list ready, you can begin to write your copy.

THE POWER OF HEADLINES

Every message must begin with a headline or its equivalent. Your headline must either convey an idea or entice the reader into wanting to learn more. Focus like a laser as you direct your headline to members of your target audience, one person at a time. Even if 50 million people read it, they'll read it one person at a time. So don't think target audience; think in terms of an individual person.

Experiment with headlines that use a news style. Experiment with headlines using all of these words—one at a time: new, announcing, presenting, and now. If possible, put a date in your headline. In radio ads or tweets, the rules about headlines apply to your first sentence.

Start your headline with a question to which the answer is "Yes." That begins the momentum. And it's all about keeping the momentum going. The more you can get people nodding, even silently, the more likely it is that they will say "Yes" when you ask them to take action.

Remember that headlines, opening lines, and subject lines create the initial bonds with your prospects. And the more connected your potential customers feel to you, the more likely they are to buy . . . and keep buying. If they feel connected, they are also much more likely to enthusiastically refer others to you.

Never forget the single most powerful word in the language of advertising: It's FREE, followed fairly closely by the word YOU. Why? Because everyone likes something for free. Including rich people. And after their own name, the sweetest sound to everyone alive is the word *you*. Take gentle hold of the reader or listener's attention by telling a story. The more personal your story, the better. Here's a secret, apparently little-known in many sectors of the advertising world: Even the biggest corporations are made up of . . . people. With names. And faces. And fascinating stories that others would like to hear.

Of course, what you have to say is important, but how you say it is equally important and, if you say it right, it's even more important. Use testimonials in your copy, as your headline or subject line. But be careful with testimonials. Don't promise results that you can't document as "typical."

A healthy mindset for copywriters is one in which you believe that the readers or viewers are going to move on to something else—anything else—unless you stop them cold. Not easy. So keep their attention. Make what they read from you the most important event of their day.

Some words are ear words—ideal for broadcast—while others are eye words that work best when being read. "Guerrilla" means one thing to the eyes, another to the ears.

THE PASSION OF GUERRILLA COPYWRITING

Traditional copywriting was about grammar, vocabulary, and spelling. Guerrilla copywriting is about motivation, persuasiveness, and passion. Don't hide your passion, excitement, and intensity from your readers. They're human, too. And once they are reminded that you are, your copy will go a lot further with them.

Verbs are very cool words to activate the mind. "Do it now." "Pay close attention." "Write better copy." "Run, don't walk." "Click here." Mark Twain was tough on copywriters. He said, "Eliminate every third word. It gives writing remarkable vigor." After trying both, Ernest Hemingway said he was convinced that copywriting was much tougher than novel writing. But we all know that the best paid of all writing is the ransom note.

Think in terms of creating original clichés: words that create obvious connections, "Like the black plague" and "Like a swarm of locusts." Make every sentence you write lead to the next sentence. This lets your copy flow all the way to the last word. Avoid rhymes and puns. They definitely are fun to write and even to read, but most of the time they are beside the point and disrupt the flow.

Also be aware that clever, overtly catchy copy smothers sales. Don't let this happen to you. The opposite of clever and catchy is compelling and conversational. Strive for that.

Readers should never talk to you about your writing; they should talk of what you're writing about.

Never use a long word when a short word will do. Never use a long sentence when you can use a short one. Never use a long paragraph, unless you want your readers to struggle through your copy.

Try to write as you speak—using contractions, sentence fragments, and informal language, especially in the area of your vocabulary. The best words are usually those in plain English.

Never forget, even for an instant, that the primary purpose of your copy is to earn a profit. Guerrilla copy is much easier to write if the starting point is an idea. If it is, trust the copy to write itself.

The purpose of guerrilla copywriting is to get people to act, using only the brute force of your ideas and words. Once you have mastered this skill, you have the ultimate leverage in business. You can attract and keep customers at lower and lower costs.

MOVING IT ONLINE

When it comes to social media and websites, you can often advertise effectively at no cost whatsoever. And with good copywriting skills, your words can spark enviable relationships— with people you have never even met.

Keep in mind everything you have learned about guerrilla copywriting when you get ready to create a website. Your domain name needs to be like your headline: compelling and memorable. Spend some time choosing several domain names and see what is available.

Then think about how your website should look; what colors and graphics should you use. How many pages should be included? What information is on the homepage? What information should be on secondary pages? How do you get readers to move from one page to another? What action do you want readers to take after they visit your site?

When you have sketched out the structure of your website and you know what you want readers to do when they visit, then you can start to create your messages. And since you already know how to create memorable copy that compels people to action, this job will be a snap.

The upcoming maneuvers are your way of stepping out into space and actually flying. We're not asking you to win awards or compliments, only to win profits for your business by tapping into the creativity you already have within you. There is no better way to ignite that creativity than to do the actual maneuver. Now go to work.

Maneuver #17
CREATE YOUR DOMAIN NAME

I want the domain name (such as www.gmarketing.com) for my site to be:

_____

_____

_____

_____

Maneuver #18
CREATE A WEBSITE

A good website provides information, offers free newsletters and other information, and even sells products and services. Most of all, it's the first crucial step in a long and mutually enjoyable relationship between you and your clients.

Your homepage—the first page people see when they visit your site—is like the window display in a store. It must be visually appealing and compelling. It must invite visitors inside to learn more. Decide why you want a website and how you can profit from it. Keep in mind that many guerrilla marketers reap great profits from sites that don't directly sell anything but merely bring them even closer to their customers. Don't forget to take full advantage of the internet's interactivity by getting your visitors actively involved. Ask them to register for something or enter a contest; this will help you get their names and contact information, as well as consent to receive more marketing from you. Getting that precious consent is one of your biggest goals. In this maneuver, you'll sketch out your site's basic idea: heading, subhead, and the key points you want to make.

(See Appendix E for **Elements of Website Design**.)

The headline on my main page is: _____

_____

My subhead is: _____

_____

My graphics are: _____

_____

_____

My colors are:_____

_____

_____

My main points are: _____

_____

_____

_____

_____

My homepage layout:

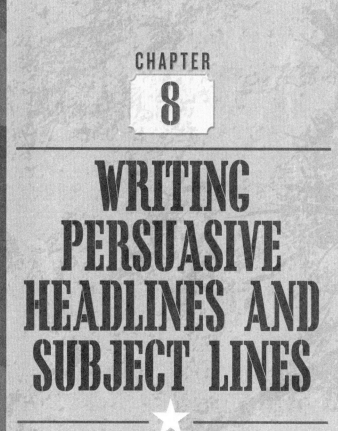

WRITING PERSUASIVE HEADLINES AND SUBJECT LINES

AT ITS CORE, MARKETING IS PERSUASION. YOU MUST persuade individuals or groups to part with one of their most prized possessions: their money.

All guerrillas know that marketing is really a high-falutin' word that means selling, and selling is a fancy word that means persuasion. If you can't persuade, you can't sell.

Many people who think they can't succeed at marketing because they can't persuade people to buy something seem to do a dandy job of persuading their spouses to be on time, their kids to do their homework, and their associates to accept an idea they've just put on the table. The moral: There are a lot of closet persuaders out there.

Guerrillas rev up their powers of persuasion with insight about their prospects and their customers, combined with intimate knowledge of their own product or service. Without those insights, you're a dead duck. With them, you're a guerrilla, poised for victory and profitability.

We'll be the first to admit that not every persuasion attempt you make will work out the way you want. But we're here to remind you of why some attempts succeed and why some fail.

Guerrillas learn from these experiences, asking themselves questions after successful persuasions: "What was the critical insight that I used?" and "How did I use it?" Of failures, they ask: "What insight should I have seen?" and "How did my attempt miss it?" Frequently, failures are caused by persuaders failing to understand the person they want to persuade. The deeper you enter into the head of your prospect, the more persuasive you will become.

8 / Writing Persuasive Headlines and Subject Lines

I t's important for you to recognize that there are different kinds of persuasion and that they have different levels of effectiveness. Gentle persuasion can be as powerful as pressured persuasion. Slow-motion persuasion works better than high-speed persuasion. All persuasion begins with connection.

So now you know the truth. There is no magic in persuasion. There is simply research time and your own energy. Back in the 1900s, ad great Claude Hopkins said (and I hope you'll excuse his sexism): "The marketing man studies the consumer. He tries to place himself in the position of the buyer. His success largely depends on doing that to the exclusion of everything else." Nothing has changed since then regarding the customer: The keys to persuasion lie in wearing the customer's shoes and seeing things through her eyes.

HEADLINES AND SUBJECT LINES

Your connections with your customers often begin with headlines and subject lines. Headlines are used in ads, commercials, telemarketing calls, direct mail letters, websites, sales presentations, and more. Can you write great ones? You know the magic words and the tragic words, but can you really write a headline or subject line that persuades people to either open your email, buy your offering, read your copy, visit your website, or call your toll-free phone number? It's not easy. But you'll know how right after you read this.

Every guerrilla destined for marketing victories knows very well that if you have ten hours to spend creating an advertisement or email, you should spend nine of them creating the headline or subject line. It's the first impression you make—often the only one—and the rest of your marketing copy will live or die by the quality of it.

Just because you don't run print ads or send emails, you can't assume that your headlines on your material is unimportant. Quite the contrary: It's crucial and can be compared to a door-to-door salesman knocking on a busy person's front door. At best you should expect that you only have time to say one thing before that person slams the door in your face or opens it widely, inviting you in.

In that brief window, you have the opportunity to tell your whole story condensed into one line or to say something so intriguing that the prospect will want to hear more. You'll have this opportunity in print ads, to be sure, but also with first lines of TV spots and radio commercials; with opening lines of letters and postcards; with first statements made by sales reps or telemarketers; in brochures and on websites; in Yellow Pages ads; in sales videos; in classified ads and infomercials; at trade shows;

and in catalogs. But today, they may first learn about you from your email subject line. People will decide to read or hear your message or to ignore you completely depending on that headline or subject line. If either is a loser, you have three strikes against you when you step up to the plate. We wish you lots of luck.

All guerrillas are delighted that today's technology makes marketing easier than ever: Websites enable them to market with even more fervor; and new software lets them create dynamite marketing materials right in their own offices. Yet no matter what technological developments arise, guerrillas never lose sight of the fact that headlines and subject lines are the cornerstones, as they dictate your positioning in your prospects' minds and determine their reaction—attention or apathy.

In print, you have one line to grab that attention. Only one line gets to be your opening line. On radio or TV, you have three seconds, and you have those same three seconds with any sales presentation or telemarketing calls. You have even less time with your subject lines on emails. Win attention and interest during that brief period or you won't win it later.

Now that we've alerted you as to the importance of headlines and subject lines, here are 20 hints to help you create winning ones:

1. Know that your opening line must either convey an idea or intrigue the reader or listener into wanting to learn more.

2. Speak directly to the reader or listener, one at a time, even if 20 million people will be exposed to your message.

3. Write your opening line in newsy style.

4. Use words that have the feeling of an important announcement.

5. Test opening lines that start with the word "announcing."

6. Test opening lines that use the word "new."

7. Put a date in your opening line.

8. Feature your price, if you're proud of it, in your opening line.

9. Feature your very easy payment plan.

10. Announce a free offer and use the word "free."

11. Offer information of value right in your opening line.

12. Start to tell a fascinating story; guerrillas know that marketing really is the truth made fascinating.

13. Begin your opening line with the words, "How to . . . "

14. Begin your opening line with "why," "which," "you," "this," "advice, or "secrets."

15. Use a testimonial style opening line.

16. Offer the reader a test.

17. Use a huge one-word headline or a very brief subject line.

18. Warn the reader not to delay buying.

19. Address your opening line to a specific person; every day there are specific individuals who want exactly what you are offering.

20. Set your headline in the largest type on the page or your opening line with your most shocking thing to say and then start your verbal or written presentations with that headline or subject line.

If the reader or listener isn't stopped by your headline or deletes your subject line, she'll move onto something else that does stop her. After all, she's looking to be stopped by something and, if it's not your message, it will be someone else's. Opening lines are your initial bonds to your prospects. And never forget for one second that the tone of your message is as important as the message itself. Bend over backwards to be believed. Whatever you do, be unique.

Boring and indirect headlines sabotage thoughtful copy and brilliant graphics every day of the year, including Christmas. Stupendous offers are overlooked by a ready public because the headline or opening line fell down on the job. There are far more terrible headlines than great ones in every edition of every newspaper and magazine—and on almost every website.

In such an atmosphere, guerrillas thrive. They love when others run opening lines that are overly cutsie and off the point. They are enthralled when competitors run ads that draw attention away from the prime offering because a copywriter wanted to make a pun or get a laugh. But you can be sure their opening lines always get noticed, generate readership, attract responses, and result in profits.

Although it's unlikely a company will achieve greatness solely based upon its headlines and opening lines, their emphasis cannot be overstated. If you don't make a solid first impression and get your foot in the door, it's unlikely you'll have any further opportunities to persuade these prospects about your remarkable products or services. Take this chance to practice writing these very important pieces.

Maneuver #19
WRITE THREE HEADLINES AND THREE SUBJECT LINES

(See Appendix F for **Headline and Copywriting Tips**.)

Three Headlines:

_____

_____

_____

Three Subject Lines:

_____

_____

_____

_____

Maneuver #20
EMAIL YOUR CUSTOMERS

Here is the assignment: Create a five-line—yes, only *five-line*—email that directs people to your website with a hyperlink. Use short, clear words and sentences and be sure to include a direct call to action, as well as clear reasons why people should visit your site or take the action you want them to take. At your site, offer a reward in return for their snail mail address or other information, if you don't have it yet. And always remember to think in terms of soft steps that build consent for more soft steps.

Subject line: _____

Copy: _____

_____

_____

_____

_____

_____

_____

_____

_____

_____

_____

_____

_____

IDENTIFYING WONDERFUL AND HORRIBLE MARKETING

★

ECAUSE MORE MARKETING FUNDS ARE INVESTED IN advertising than any other weapon—and because an embarrassingly huge amount of that investment is just plain wasted—marketing guerrillas recognize several important truths about copy and graphics.

Ten things advertising copy should always be:

1. Readable
2. Informative
3. Clear
4. Honest
5. Simple
6. Strategic
7. Motivating
8. Competitive
9. Specific
10. Believable

Ten things not to do with advertising graphics:

1. Don't let the art overpower the idea.
2. Don't let the art overpower the headline.
3. Don't let the art overpower the copy.
4. Don't let the art fail to advance the sale.
5. Don't let the art fail to grab casual readers or viewers.
6. Don't let the art fail to get the ad or spot noticed.
7. Don't let the art fail to be different.
8. Don't let the art be created in a hurry.
9. Don't let the art fight the product's identity.
10. Don't let the art dominate the ad.

Guerrillas are also fascinated by the failures of advertising and know the main reasons why so much of it falls short, so we've provided a list for this as well.

Top 25 Reasons Advertising Fails

1. Premature abandonment
2. Silly positioning
3. Failure to focus
4. Starting without a plan
5. Picking the wrong media for the right audience
6. Picking the right media for the wrong audience
7. Being unclear to prospects
8. Not understanding customers
9. Not understanding self
10. Exaggeration that undermines truth
11. Not keeping up with change
12. Unrealistic expectations
13. Overspending or underspending
14. Saving money in the wrong places
15. Inattention to tiny, but nuclear-powered, details
16. Missing the point about profitability
17. Thinking it can be done without hard work
18. Unimpressive first impressions
19. Committees and layers of management
20. Not using media to their greatest advantage
21. Not supporting advertising with other marketing
22. Starting out in the wrong direction
23. Allowing success to beget lethargy
24. Judging the future by the past
25. Boring advertising

Maneuver #21
DRAFT A BROCHURE

You may need a written brochure right now, and there's a good chance that you'll need a digital brochure either now or later. Remember that print and electronic brochures are great places to include all the details. Will it be bifold or trifold? Why?

My Brochure Layout:

Maneuver #22
CREATE A MAGAZINE AD

You may never run a full-page ad in a magazine, but this maneuver is still superb discipline for you because, as a guerrilla, you know that the idea is king. Creating the ad means describing the visuals, designing the page, and writing the headline, subhead, and copy.

The headline is: _____

_____

_____

My subhead is: _____

_____

_____

My graphics are: _____

Maneuver #23
CREATE A 30-SECOND RADIO SPOT

This assignment involves writing a script for a 30-second radio commercial, which ought to be between 50 and 70 words maximum. Consider: Do you want music? If so, what kind? Sound effects? Should there be a male announcer, female announcer, or several voices? Be specific. Be sure to mention not only the product or service, but also exactly what you want the listener to do. What radio brings to the party is intimacy, so capitalize upon that particular strength when you create your commercial. Keep in mind that listeners will hear it over and over again. OK . . . start writing.

MAKING YOUR BUSINESS A TV STAR

K NOW THIS: TO MAKE A BUSINESS A TV STAR, A guerrilla thinks in terms of profits instead of plaudits. Guerrillas think of substance before style.

Because we're smack dab in the middle of The Information Age, and time is so darned important, guerrillas do not bombard prospects and customers with gimmicks and pizzazz. Instead, they honor their time with beneficial information and solid content. The substance of their advertising is so lush, yet concise, that substance becomes their style.

Is your current marketing distinctive because of its style or because of its substance? The ideal answer should be *both*. Your stylish flair conveys your identity and captures the attention of your targeted audience. Substance, on the other hand, makes essential points, offers a takeaway for viewers, and motivates that audience to take action.

Well-informed advertisers ensure that both their style and substance are obvious, and that their product or service always has the starring role in all marketing efforts. We've all had the experience of viewing a TV spot or reading an ad and wondering what the heck it was talking about, so you know what we're getting at.

In the early days of marketing, nobody needed special effects. When Harley Procter and his cousin, James Gamble, churned their soap too long and it floated, they came out and said Ivory is the soap that floats. Later, stressing its purity, they said it was 99 and 44/100ths percent pure. People knew exactly what they meant.

But now the creative revolution is upon us. In the name of *creativity*—rather than the less glamorous but more accurate name of *selling*—billions of dollars are being wasted each year. That's a conservative estimate.

The creative rebels—many of whom are no doubt award-winners—can't help get carried away by style, and in the melee, substance gets lost. Marketing is definitely not a shuck and jive show or an entertainment medium. Its purpose is selling, and it should therefore be loaded with substance.

In the 1950s, Alka Seltzer produced a series of dynamite TV spots. Everyone seemed to love them. But Alka Seltzer sales tanked. There is no correlation between customers liking your marketing and buying what it promotes.

You can be sure that the top salespeople in the world don't begin their presentations with a tap dance or a cartwheel. They succeed because they exhaustively prepare for the sales

Be on guard against the multitude of "creative" people who populate the marketing profession. Too many of them have been trained to create a gorgeous picture, a rhyming headline, or a flashing website when they should be trying to create an eye-popping upswing in your sales curve. Remember, if creative ideas cost more than they earn for you, something is wrong with the equation. The equation should read: "creativity equals profits."

10 / Making Your Business a TV Star

meeting, learning about the customers' needs and then offering their companies' products or services to provide appropriate solutions. If the presentations happen to be well designed in PowerPoint, that's fine—as long as the bells and whistles don't overwhelm the promise.

The overriding concept in your marketing should be to *present substance* and do it with style. Note that the emphasis is on the substance, which is what viewers will remember.

There is no better way to communicate both substance and style than through TV commercials. Although it's true that the internet continues to grow and someday will likely end up being the most important way to reach your marketplace, that day is not yet with us. Until that time comes, TV continues to reign supreme in the marketing spectrum.

Here are the main reasons why this is true:

★ *TV*—especially cable—now allows you to target your audience more precisely than you could in the past. It allows you to single out specific groups of people, such as businesspeople, and even hone in on selected neighborhoods in your community.

★ *TV advertising* is now more affordable than it ever has been, in many cases lower in cost than radio. Direct response companies are discovering that there is a 24-hour viewing audience out there with even lower rates, and there are program-length infomercials that cost what regular one-minute spots used to cost. Again, we tip our hats to the cable industry for putting TV advertising within everybody's reach.

REMEMBER THESE FACTS TO PRODUCE A WINNER

Now we're going to reveal some secrets that can help you produce a winning TV commercial for your business:

★ *TV can be inexpensive, if done right.* The cost to run commercials is no more than $20 during prime time in most markets in the United States. The cost to produce a commercial, although over $200,000 during 2011, should run you no more than $1,000. You don't need Tiger or Serena or Lady Gaga endorsing what you have to offer. You're after sales, not celebs or Emmys.

★ *TV is a visual medium.* Don't think of it as a radio spot with pictures. Think of it as a place to tell a visual story with a beginning, a middle, and an end. More than 70 percent of us mute the commercials with our remote zappers, which means that if you're not telling your story and saying your name visually, you're not telling your story or saying your name at all.

★ *TV is powered by an idea.* Forget the special effects, music, staging, and lighting. First think of the idea. That's what makes a commercial successful—a strong offer, a visual expression of a good idea. Once you have the idea, everything else will fall into place. Without the idea, your commercial has hardly any chance of success.

★ *Special effects can overwhelm your commercial.* Many people get carried away at their chance to be like Steven Spielberg and fall prey to gizmos and gimmicks. Use special effects only to highlight and further convey your idea. Otherwise, they act like vampires, sucking attention away from your offer.

★ *TV doesn't cost as little as you think.* A few paragraphs ago, we told you that TV advertising is inexpensive. Now here we are telling you that it might be expensive. We recognize the seeming conflict and will explain. The spots are inexpensive. The production can be inexpensive. But you've got to run several spots every day, several days a week, three weeks out of four, and for a minimum of three months—unless you're making a direct response offer—before you see any glimmer of success. If you're looking for instant gratification, look somewhere other than the tube.

★ *TV is made better if you operate from a script.* You need not waste your precious money having somebody produce a storyboard for you because you don't need one. But you do need a script that tells the exact visuals and the exact sounds that will go on screen for 30 seconds.

★ *TV production costs are lower when you preproduce with care.* The way guerrillas cut 200,000 ugly dollars from their TV production costs is by having preproduction meetings where all production details are handled. These are followed by rehearsals for the talent and the technicians. There should be zero surprises on the day of the TV shooting.

★ *TV production costs are lowered still if you produce your soundtrack first.* Once you have it, you can shoot footage to match the amount of time the words and music take. Shooting sound and picture at the same time means that if a plane flies overhead or a motorcycle zooms by, you need to reshoot. Do your sound first, using professionals, then shoot the visuals.

★ *TV's greatest strength is its ability to demonstrate.* Newspapers report the news. Magazines involve readers. Radio provides intimacy. Direct response adds urgency. The power of TV lies in the way it can demonstrate. It can show before and after, with a shot of the product in use during the middle. It can target left- and right-brained people. It can combine all the art forms into a masterful blending of show and sell.

Despite all these advantages, TV commercials can quickly become duds if you are not careful. These are the top ten things that can turn a TV commercial into a loser:

1. It is more entertaining than motivating.

2. It is not clear about its promise.

3. It is not visual but depends on words.

4. It is schlocky, lacking in credibility.

5. It is high pressure or exaggerated.

6. It is a fabulous film but a terrible commercial.

7. It is so clever you forget who ran it.

8. It is so wrapped up in special effects, it's devoid of an idea.

9. It is too complex for an idea to come shining through.

10. It is boring, boring, boring.

Now for the top ten things that make a TV commercial a winner:

1. It is clear about its competitive advantage.

2. It is clear about its promise.

3. It is intensely visual.

4. It is professional looking.

5. It is believable and credible.

6. It creates a powerful desire.

7. It is focused on advancing the sale, not being clever.

8. It is wrapped up with the product.

9. It demonstrates the benefit.

10. It is fascinating even the tenth time you see it.

A final word: Just as being online doesn't mean beans unless your website is part of a well-crafted marketing program, being on TV is also no guarantee of profitability. TV commercials must be part of a marketing program and supported with other media.

Never forget that somebody once defined a TV commercial as "a dream interrupter." Try this Maneuver to create commercials that I won't mind interrupting my dreams.

★

Maneuver #24
CREATE A 30-SECOND TV COMMERCIAL

You now know that TV remains the champion of marketing and that professional commercials can be very cheap, if done right. Here's your chance to create a script for your own commercial. You have 30 seconds to put your message across. Many people mute the sound during commercials, so remember that your message cannot depend on audio.

Your Script:

Video	Audio

Video	Audio

CHAPTER

11

MAKING AN IMPACT IN YOUR COMMUNITY

★

UERRILLAS KNOW WELL THAT PEOPLE ALWAYS PREFER to do business with friends instead of strangers. You must, therefore, learn about your community and get involved in helping people in it. They, in turn, become involved by helping you. Friendships are made while you are helping them or they are helping you.

From these friends come business associates, marketing partners, investors, employees, customers, prospects, suppliers, and referrals.

Becoming involved with the community entails more than joining clubs. Instead of thinking only about what clubs or organizations you can join, consider contributing your brains and energy to the community and working hard to make it a better place. By doing this, you prove your conscientiousness and display your noble efforts with the work you do instead of the words you say.

One of the keys to marketing in your community is establishing relationships. You do this by serving on committees, going to Little League games, helping set up parades, organizing holiday decorating programs, and serving in a million other ways. When people see you in action serving others, they'll regard you as a person of action, someone who can be trusted. So when those people hear you say something in a marketing context, they will tend to believe you. When you make an offer, they know it's not going to be bogus. You've proven yourself in the community.

There are wrong ways to demonstrate community involvement as well. If you volunteer to work on a committee but are never available for meetings, or if you sponsor a Little League team and don't show up for games, you're proving yourself to be crass and superficial. People will view you as sucking up the community to get business, instead of contributing to it for altruistic reasons.

Consumers are more sophisticated than ever these days. They recognize the difference between serving the community and serving yourself. If you're not willing to devote honest time and energy to community efforts, then don't even pick up this weapon. It will backfire.

Your community is not defined by mere geography. Digital communities are springing up all over the place as the world goes online. Whatever the size or scope of your community, the guerrilla rule remains the same: Do unto others as they hope you will do unto them. Community groups—whether they are virtual or in your neighborhood—are looking for your help, not your hype.

While you're involved with your community, be sure that you're attuned to its members' problems. Listen for the *ouch*.

Guerrillas know that it's easier to sell the solution to a problem than to sell a positive benefit. For this reason, guerrillas position their companies to be ace problem-solvers—especially during tough times. They hone in on the problems confronting their prospects or their community members, then offer products or services as solutions. Almost all individuals and companies are beset with problems of one sort or another. Your job is to spot those problems, and that's easier to do when you are involved in people's lives.

Networking is not a time to toot your own trombone, but to ask questions, listen carefully to the answers, and keep your marketing radar attuned to detect the presence of problems. You can also learn of problems that require solving at trade shows, professional association meetings, prospect questionnaires, and even sales calls.

GO VIRTUAL!

As important as it is to participate in your physical community, it may be even more important these days to engage in virtual communities, especially if your business does not rely on your neighbors to be your customers. Participation in virtual communities can come in many forms: placing banner ads on websites; featuring links to associates' pages on your website; posting articles of relevance to online groups; joining chats; sending or following tweets; or simply clicking "Like" on various social media pages, such as on Facebook and LinkedIn. Social media can also be a great place for *crowdsourcing*—rallying people around a cause or event to spark awareness and often raise much-needed funds for a nonprofit.

There are many advantages to being part of virtual communities. By investing a little time and small amounts of money, you can link your company name with a wide range of powerful online communities in your business area. Depending on what type of business you offer, you can continue to focus your efforts locally or branch out nationally or even internationally, simply by getting customers' attention and gaining trust through a click of the "Like" button. Potential customers you may never even have considered might see your support and become interested in your business in unexpected ways.

Explore these virtual opportunities as much as possible and you will reap the rewards. As mobile devices continue to permeate every aspect of our business landscape, it becomes even easier to get involved at your leisure—and even more possible to get noticed in just the blink of an eye. Who knows? The next tweet you send could go viral among followers, and suddenly you'll have a thriving online community of your own.

Maneuver #25
HELP YOUR COMMUNITY

1. Make a list of the organizations you can become involved with, both community and online groups. List the things you can do for each group. Don't offer to do anything that you can't accomplish with excellence. So be selective.

_____

_____

_____

_____

2. Make a phone call, send a letter, or send an email volunteering your services. Take the time below to list who you'll call, who you'll write, and who you'll email. _____

_____

_____

_____

_____

3. Create a proposal for the single best prospect of all. Next, knock yourself out making the proposal. _____

_____

_____

_____

_____

_____

_____

4. Make a list of prospects in your community who have not yet been converted to customers. Then, select the ten who have potential to be the most profitable for your business. Pull out all the stops when contacting these ten and learn what works for you and what doesn't. _____

_____

_____

_____

_____

_____

_____

_____

_____

_____

5. Put in writing a list of the ways you offer remarkable service. The longer your list, the easier it will be for you to thrive during a poor economy. Augment that list by adding three items of service that you have not stressed before.

When all else is equal, the company that offers the best services is the one that will win the customer. Now, post that list on your website. Market it to your community.

_____

_____

_____

_____

_____

6. List the technologies you employ to render superlative service: email, fax machine, voice mail, Facebook, Twitter, auto-responder, toll-free number, cell phone, pager, sales funnel—so that you can make customer contact as simple as possible. Be sure you have a content-rich website that sees things from the customer's point of view. Easy? No. Mandatory? Yes. Few people know your community as well as you. _____

_____

_____

_____

_____

_____

_____

Maneuver #26
CREATE A REFERRAL PLAN

While helping your community, you will make contacts. After you
have converted some of those contacts to customers, you want
to deliberately create processes so that those customers can help
you get new customers. Guerrillas know that existing customers
are the best source of new customers. They aren't shy about
coming right out and asking for referrals. The best times to ask for
referrals are immediately after the sale, six months later, and one
year later. The most successful—meaning profitable—companies
have comprehensive referral plans with one or more people in
charge of implementing/administering the plan and assigned
dates for obtaining referrals during every year.

My referral plan is:

_____

★

Maneuver #27
PLAN FOR GUERRILLA FOLLOW-UP

Fervent follow-up is even more important than a referral plan because selling to existing customers is much easier than selling to new customers—and far more lucrative over the long run. Most customers appreciate check-ins and follow-up; these simple steps demonstrate that you are thinking about them and care. The maneuver below helps you create an effective follow-up strategy.

My follow-up plan is:

Time After Purchase	Specific Follow-Up	Action

ENSURING YOUR VICTORY

★

YOU ARE SURROUNDED. ALL AROUND YOU ARE ENEMIES vying for the same prize. They're out to get your customers and your prospects—the good and honest people who ought to be buying what you're selling. These enemies are disguised as owners of small and medium-sized businesses.

Several of the enemies are grossly larger than you. Some have the power and personality of Godzilla. Many of them are far better funded than you. Some have been successfully operating their businesses for decades and have a significant dedicated customer base they've built up over the years. Some may have jumped out ahead of you with investments in emerging digital tools and savvy social marketing techniques.

These enemies thrive on competition. They're out to get you and get you good. They're out for the disposable income currently held by your prospective and past customers. They're out for the attention of every red-blooded consumer who goes online, "checks in" at an establishment, reads the newspaper, checks a magazine, listens to the radio, watches TV, or grabs a handful of junk mail out of the mailbox. And don't forget the floods of email.

Your enemies mean business: *your* business, *your* profits. Some of them can post more online banner ads, blast out more emails, and run more commercials than you'll ever produce. They can outspend you in every arena of marketing that money can buy. But it's equally as important to know that they *can't* outspend you in marketing arenas that money *can't* buy. If you exert the time, the energy, and the information, you can gain marketing leverage over your enemies without putting up megabucks.

EMERGING TOOLS TO BREAK THE COMPETITION

Marketing continues to get increasingly more sophisticated, especially when it comes to social media. You need to be aware of all of these emerging tools, see if or how your competition uses them, and decide if they can be advantageous to your business.

★ *Search engine optimization (SEO).* Every company wants to be discovered first when customers search online, such as through Google. Taking advantage of SEO is how marketers try to influence the results or the algorithms created by the search engines. As these become more and more sophisticated, it becomes increasingly important for marketers to focus on content that is rich, authentic, and appropriate to the search, rather than adding a few key unrelated words that might draw readers into the site but annoy them as soon as they realize how you tricked them into coming there.

★ *Influence score.* Today, customers rely on authorities who are genuinely "in the know." If you are selecting an online brand spokesperson—or are looking for a customer who can bring in other customers to shout about your product or service—you want someone who has a great deal of influence within that community. Companies such as Klout now actually measure those scores, assigning a number to those individuals who have the most influence.

★ *Location-based marketing.* Many companies are now using social media tools to find customers who use mobile devices to locate good deals and bargains while on the go. These location-based technologies, such as those offered by foursquare, encourage customers to "check in" at locations to find bargains or just to let their friends know where they are. If you have a brick-and-mortar business, using these services can be a great way to bring in new customers and create brand loyalty.

★ *Video marketing.* It's now estimated that Americans watch more than 1.3 billion videos online every day. YouTube has become a top online destination not just for popular entertainment content, but also for companies to post innovative video messages that engage and inform new and old customers. Such efforts need to be kept brief (under 60 seconds, if that long) and offer customers prescriptive content; if the video feels like a commercial, your customers will click off.

★ *Gaming.* Some experts believe that gaming as a marketing trend will grow to nearly $3 billion by 2016. Gaming isn't just a teen fixation; the age range continues to widen, and customers enjoy playing games even as they are trying to solve problems in business and at home.

★ *Apps.* Apps can be a fun way to engage customers, but caution must be exercised. While it's estimated that apps have been downloaded nearly 11 billion times, a large portion of the 300,000 apps in existence have failed. This is some cause for concern, as apps can be expensive to create, and the prices for downloading continue to drop.

The digital landscape continues to change at a frenetic rate, and it's critical that you keep a close eye on your competitors' efforts. You don't want to be left behind if your customers start to "check in" elsewhere; on the other hand, you don't want to invest all of your marketing resources creating YouTube videos that no one watches.

To summarize, here are ten attitudes you should now include in your guerrilla arsenal.

1. You've got to open your mind to the full extent of marketing, including all avenues of digital media. It's fuller than you thought.
2. You've got to adopt the personality of other successful guerrilla marketers. Without it, life will be tough.
3. You've got to think about marketing differently. A lot of the old truths have turned into myths. And even the best of them did not include the internet or social media in their formulas.
4. You've got to follow an easy-to-understand, easy-to-follow battle strategy when planning your guerrilla marketing attack.

5. You've got to define what you want your attack to accomplish with precision and realism. If you're not defining, you're not attacking.

6. You've got to attack—do exactly what your plan said you'd do. You must take action.

7. You've got to understand which media can best serve your needs—and whether or not you need traditional media at all.

8. You've got to orient everything about your business to your customer—that person above all who can help you prosper. Your customer must sense your dedication.

9. You've got to recognize the fast-changing nature of marketing today. It's wilder than ever, but you can master it if you keep up with it. Guerrillas do.

10. You've got to maintain your guerrilla marketing attack. You can fulfill the other nine requirements superbly, but if you don't fulfill this one, you're a goner.

★

Maneuver #28
TAKE SPECIFIC ACTION

This is where the rubber meets the road. You must take action now if you really want to achieve the spectacular profits you've been dreaming about. This is the single most important maneuver because nothing will happen without it.

Below, list actions you are planning to take along with completion dates. At least half of the concepts must address competition and factor in social media techniques mentioned in this chapter.

Do	By

Maneuver #29
ACTIVATE YOUR ATTACK

After you have planned how you will attack your competition, you need to activate your attack. Take a look at these ten steps to help your guerrilla marketing attack succeed, and then use the space on the next page to plan the steps you will take to activate your attack.

Ten steps to make your guerrilla marketing attack a success:

1. Research market, product, media, competition, industry, prospects, customers, technology, benefits, the internet.
2. Write benefits list and select or identify your competitive advantages, as explained in Maneuvers #2 and #3.
3. Select marketing weapons.
4. Create marketing plan focus with seven sentences, as explained in Maneuver #6.
5. Make guerrilla marketing calendar as explained in Maneuver #10.
6. Find fusion marketing partners with the same prospects; see Maneuver #9 for details.
7. Launch in slow motion; make sure you are comfortable both financially and emotionally with your attack.

8. Maintain attack. Most money is lost when guerrillas fail to keep the pressure on.

9. Keep track: know when you hit the bull's-eye and when you miss.

10. Keep up with new techniques in all areas: social media, message, media, budget, results.

Using those ten tips and all the information you have learned in this book, put your action plan into writing. Decide on the priority order of your weapons' launches and include specific launch dates and the people who will be responsible for them.

What Launched	When	Who

What Launched	When	Who

Maneuver #30
RECEIVE YOUR MARCHING ORDERS

You have already completed most of the necessary components for your guerrilla marketing attack. Now all you need to do is create and review your final checklist so you're sure you're ready to go.

For this one final maneuver, time is far less important than honesty. If you answer YES to all ten questions, you're ready and cleared for takeoff. If not, then you need to go back and fill in the missing ingredients right now. Be honest, because the only person you cheat by being dishonest is yourself.

1. I completed all the maneuvers in this battle plan and believe that my answers are thorough and accurate:

   ❑ **YES**   ❑ **NO**

2. I have at least one clear and compelling competitive advantage:

   ❑ **YES**   ❑ **NO**

3. My marketing weapons are selected, prioritized, and assigned to a responsible person for action:

   ❑ **YES**   ❑ **NO**

4. I have a seven-sentence marketing plan and am confident that it will be effective:

   ❑ **YES**   ❑ **NO**

5. My guerrilla marketing calendar is complete for the first 12 months:

   ❑ **YES**   ❑ **NO**

6. I have selected my fusion marketing partners:

   ❑ **YES**   ❑ **NO**

7. I have launch dates for each of my weapons and will proceed in slow motion:

   ❏ **YES** ❏ **NO**

8. I am committed to maintaining my guerrilla marketing attack:

   ❏ **YES** ❏ **NO**

9. I will measure all results and grade myself honestly each month:

   ❏ **YES** ❏ **NO**

10. I will constantly strive to improve the effectiveness of my guerrilla marketing attack:

   ❏ **YES** ❏ **NO**

If you answered YES to all ten questions, then you are ready to launch your marketing attack.

CHARGE!

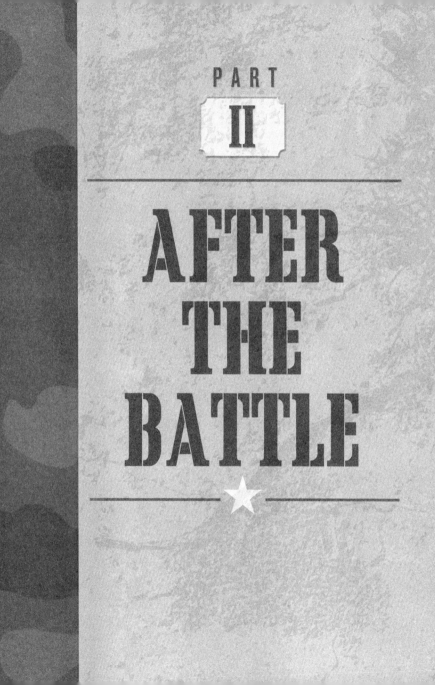

PART

II

AFTER THE BATTLE

CHAPTER 13

DEBRIEFING

★

Y OU HAVE NOW BEEN ARMED WITH THE ACUMEN
and savvy to triumph over any competition, to
prosper in any economic climate. You have been
provided with insight into more weapons than your
competition will ever have—regardless of their size. As
a guerrilla marketer, you have the depth of information

required for success in any marketplace. You have the all-important momentum. Some may outspend you; none will outthink you.

We created this battle plan with one thing in mind: your profitability. Sure, we wanted you to enjoy yourself and retain balance in your life. But underneath it all, we have planned for your financial reward. You now know about planning. You know about doing. You know about your strengths. You know about your limitations. Now, as a guerrilla, you have reached that next level. You will thrive in this position because you've now got the skill, the talent, and the insights to carry you upward and onward forever. All you need now is the commitment—that is what will help you achieve momentum and continued results.

You have learned timeless information that will carry you exactly where you want to go. We congratulate you on completing the battle plan that is dedicated to taking you there. But never forget that this battle plan is not about the answers that you give. It's about actions that you take.

PART

III

APPENDICES

200 GUERRILLA MARKETING WEAPONS

★

Maxi-Media

1. Advertising
2. Direct mail
3. Newspaper ads
4. Radio spots
5. Magazine ads
6. Billboards
7. TV commercials

Mini-Media

8. Marketing plans
9. Marketing calendars
10. Identity

11. Business cards
12. Stationery
13. Personal letters
14. Telephone marketing
15. Toll-free number
16. Vanity phone number
17. Yellow Pages
18. Postcards
19. Postcard decks
20. Classified ads
21. Per-order, per-inquiry advertising
22. Free ads in shoppers
23. Circulars, fliers
24. Community bulletin boards
25. Movie ads
26. Outside signs
27. Street banners
28. Window displays
29. Inside signs
30. Posters
31. Canvassing
32. Door hangers
33. Elevator pitches
34. Value story
35. Back-end sales
36. Letters of recommendation
37. Attendance at trade shows

E- Media

38. Computer
39. Printer, fax
40. Chat rooms
41. Forums boards
42. Internet bulletin boards
43. List-building
44. Personalized emails
45. Email signatures
46. Canned emails
47. Bulk emails
48. Audio/video postcards
49. Domain names
50. Websites
51. Landing pages
52. Merchant accounts

53. Shopping carts
54. Auto-responders
55. Search-engine rankings
56. Electronic brochures
57. RSS feeds
58. Blogs
59. Podcasting
60. Own ezine publications
61. Ads in other ezines
62. Ebooks
63. Content for other web-sites
64. Webinar productions
65. Joint ventures
66. Word-of-mouse marketing
67. Viral marketing
68. eBay, other auction sites
69. Click analyzers
70. Pay-per-click ads
71. Search-engine keywords
72. Google AdWords
73. Sponsored links
74. Reciprocal link exchanges
75. Banner exchanges
76. Web conversion rates

Info Media

77. Knowledge of your market
78. Research studies
79. Specific customer data
80. Case studies
81. Sharing
82. Brochures
83. Catalogs
84. Business directories
85. Public service announcements
86. Newsletters
87. Speeches
88. Free consultations
89. Free demonstrations
90. Free seminars
91. Published articles
92. Published columns
93. Published books
94. Publishing-on-demand items

95. Speaker at clubs
96. Teleseminars
97. Infomercials
98. Constant learning

Human Media

99. Marketing insights
100. Yourself
101. Your employees and reps
102. Designated guerrillas
103. Employee attire
104. Social demeanor
105. Target audiences
106. Your own circle of influence
107. Contact time with customers
108. How you say hello and goodbye
109. Teaching ability
110. Stories
111. Sales training
112. Use of downtime
113. Networking
114. Professional titles

115. Affiliate marketing
116. Media contacts
117. "A" list customers
118. Core story
119. Sense of urgency
120. Limited offers
121. Calls to action
122. Satisfied customers

Non-Media

123. Benefits lists
124. Competitive advantages
125. Gifts
126. Service
127. Public relations
128. Fusion marketing
129. Bartering
130. Word-of-mouth
131. Buzz
132. Community involvement
133. Club and association memberships
134. Free directory listings
135. Trade show booths
136. Special events

137. Name tags at events
138. Luxury box at events
139. Gift certificates
140. Audio-visual aids
141. Flipcharts
142. Reprints and blowups
143. Coupons
144. Free-trial offers
145. Guarantees
146. Contests and sweep-
     stakes
147. Baking or craft abilities
148. Lead buying
149. Follow-up
150. Tracking plans
151. Marketing-on-hold
152. Branded entertainment
153. Product placement
154. Radio talk show guest
155. TV talk show guest
156. Subliminal marketing

Company Attributes

157. Proper view of marketing
158. Brand-name awareness

159. Positioning
160. Name
161. Meme
162. Theme line
163. Writing ability
164. Copywriting ability
165. Headline copy
166. Location
167. Hours of operation
168. Days of operation
169. Credit cards accepted
170. Financing available
171. Credibility
172. Reputation
173. Efficiency
174. Quality
175. Service
176. Selection
177. Price
178. Opportunities to
     upgrade
179. Referral program
180. Spying
181. Testimonials
182. Extra value

183. Adopt noble cause

Company Attitudes

184. Easy to do business with
185. Honest interest in people
186. Telephone demeanor
187. Passion and enthusiasm
188. Sensitivity
189. Patience
190. Flexibility
191. Generosity

192. Self-confidence
193. Neatness
194. Aggressiveness
195. Competitiveness
196. High energy
197. Speed
198. Ability to focus
199. Attention to details
200. Readiness to take action

GUERRILLA SOCIAL MEDIA WEAPONS

★

Hardware

- · Smartphone with a data plan
- · Notebook computer
- · Video camera
- · Digital camera

- Good microphone
- Boingo Wifi membership
- Webcam

Software

- Graphic and photo editing software
- Audio editing software
- Video editing software
- Software to manage contacts and customer relations
- Browser with social media and Google plug-ins

Social Networking

Facebook

- Facebook profile
- Facebook pages
- Facebook groups
- Facebook events
- Facebook applications

LinkedIn

- LinkedIn profile
- LinkedIn slideshare
- LinkedIn Google presentations
- LinkedIn Twitter
- LinkedIn blog import
- LinkedIn groups
- LinkedIn answers

· LinkedIn events

Other Sites

· Orkut
· Google+
· Hi5
· Xing
· Ecademy
· Brazen Careerist

Self-Branded Networks

· Ning
· BuddyPress
· Jive Software
· Pluck
· Awareness Inc.
· Acquia
· Drupal

Nanoblogging Weapons

· Twitter
· Complete Twitter profile
· Public Twitter lists
· Private Twitter lists
· Status updates
· FriendFeed
· URL shorteners, such as Bit.ly and Ow.ly

Third-Party Social Networking Applications

- TweetDeck
- HootSuite
- SocialToo
- Seesmic
- Ping.fm

Photo Sharing

- Dropbox
- Flickr
- Picasa
- Pinterest
- Instagram

Document Sharing

- Dropbox
- SlideShare
- Scribd

Audio and Video

- Podcasts
- YouTube
- Viddler
- Niche and specialty networks
  - Vimeo
  - FameCast
  - blip.tv

- – Facebook video
- – Strutta

Real-Time Social Media

- · Ustream
- · Justin.tv
- · Skype
- · CoveritLive
- · Tinychat

Webcasts and Web Conferencing

- · GoToMeeting
- · WebEx
- · Screencast.com
- · Your website
- · Forums
- · Microsites
- · Your blog

WordPress, Self-Hosted Blog Sites, and Weapons

- · WordPress.com
- · WordPress.org
- · WordPress themes

Plug-Ins

- · All in One SEO
- · ShareThis

- Tweet This
- Google Sitemap Generator
- PowerPress
- Google Analytics
- WPtouch
- WP-o-Matic
- Akismet
- WP to Twitter
- WordPress.com Stats
- Commenting system
- Disqus
- IntenseDebate

Content Management Systems (CMS)

- Joomla!
- Drupal
- Mambo
- Ubertor (real estate)
- RSS feeds
- Feedblitz
- Yahoo Pipes
- Wikis

Light Blogging Tools

- Tumblr
- Posterous

Social Bookmarking

- Digg
- StumbleUpon
- Reddit
- Delicious

Mobile and Location-Based Tools

- foursquare
- Facebook Mobile
- Qik

Guerrilla Intelligence Tools

- search.twitter.com
  By words
  By language
  People
  Within a specific distance
  Dates
  By attitudes
  Containing links
  Including re-Tweets
- Twitter Grader
- BackType
- BackTweets
- Twellow
- Radian 6

Guerrilla Management
- Biz360 community
- Twazzup
- Google Analytics
- Payment systems

Directories
- Blog directories
- Podcast directories
- iTunes
- Twitter directories

The Major Directories
- Klout
- Twellow
- Twibes
- WeFollow
- Twitterholic

Google Weapons
- Google apps
- Google+
- Gmail for business
- Google calendar
- Google docs
- Google groups
- Google sites secure

- Google video
- Google profiles
- Google friend connect
- Google wave
- Google alerts
- Google feed reader
- Google feed bundles
- Google buzz

Email

- Your email signature
- Email newsletter

List Management Software

- AWeber
- Constant Contact

Event Marketing Tools

- Meetup
- Eventbrite
- Tweetup organizing sites

Cutting-Edge Weapons

- Augmented reality applications
- Social CRM
- Smartphone payment systems

APPENDIX C

THE TOP TEN MARKETING MEMES

★

SOME OF THE BEST-LOVED AD IMAGES OF THE 20TH century had names like Tony, Betty, and Ronald, according to *Advertising Age*. Others, like the Marlboro Man, were not exactly beloved, but there is no denying that the guy on the horse had tremendous worldwide impact as he became an instant identifier of Philip Morris Co.'s Marlboro cigarettes.

From frozen vegetables to automobile tires, these types of carefully drawn characters helped their brands become dominant in their fields. According to a 1999 *Advertising Age* article, many of the most famous ad icons were the brainchild of Chicago-based Leo Burnett Co., under the creative direction of people like Jay Conrad Levinson, who specialized in building brands through the use of enormously popular characters.

The list below is *Advertising Age's* list of the Top Ten ad memes of the 20th century. The magazine chose memes that had a powerful impact on their market and made its selections based on effectiveness, longevity, recognizability, and cultural impact.

1. The Marlboro Man, Marlboro cigarettes
2. Ronald McDonald, McDonald's restaurants
3. The Green Giant, Green Giant vegetables
4. Betty Crocker, Betty Crocker food products
5. The Energizer Bunny, Eveready Energizer batteries
6. The Pillsbury Doughboy, assorted Pillsbury foods
7. Aunt Jemima, Aunt Jemima pancake mixes and syrup
8. The Michelin Man, Michelin tires
9. Tony the Tiger, Kellogg's Sugar Frosted Flakes
10. Elsie, Borden dairy products

TOP SLOGANS, JINGLES, AND AD CAMPAIGNS

★

IN MARCH 1999, *ADVERTISING AGE* INCLUDED A SPECIAL section on advertising in the 20th century. Included in that section were these next three lists of what the magazine decided were the century's Top Ten Slogans (along with five honorable mentions), Top Ten Jingles, and Top 100 Advertising Campaigns.

Top Ten Slogans of the 20th Century

1. Diamonds are forever (DeBeers)
2. Just do it (Nike)
3. The pause that refreshes (Coca-Cola)
4. Tastes great, less filling (Miller Lite)
5. We try harder (Avis)
6. Good to the last drop (Maxwell House)
7. Breakfast of champions (Wheaties)
8. Does she . . . or doesn't she? (Clairol)
9. When it rains it pours (Morton Salt)
10. Where's the beef? (Wendy's)

Honorable Mentions

- Look Ma, no cavities! (Crest toothpaste)
- Let your fingers do the walking (Yellow Pages)
- Loose lips sink ships (public service)
- M&Ms melt in your mouth, not in your hand (M&M candies)
- We bring good things to life (General Electric)

Top 10 Jingles of the 20th Century

1. You deserve a break today (McDonald's)
2. Be all that you can be (U.S. Army)
3. Pepsi-Cola hits the spot (Pepsi-Cola)
4. Mmm, mmm good (Campbell)
5. See the USA in your Chevrolet (GM)

6. I wish I was an Oscar Mayer Wiener (Oscar Mayer)

7. Double your pleasure, double your fun (Wrigley's Doublemint gum)

8. Winston tastes good like a cigarette should (Winston)

9. It's the real thing (Coca-Cola)

10. A little dab'll do ya (Brylcreem)

Top 100 Advertising Campaigns

1. Volkswagen, "Think small," Doyle Dane Bernbach, 1959

2. Coca-Cola, "The pause that refreshes," D'Arcy Co., 1940

3. Marlboro, "The Marlboro Man," Leo Burnett Co., 1955

4. Nike, "Just do it," Wieden & Kennedy, 1988

5. McDonald's, "You deserve a break today," Needham, Harper & Steers, 1971

6. DeBeers, "A diamond is forever," N.W. Ayer & Son, 1948

7. Absolut Vodka, "The Absolut Bottle," TBWA, 1981

8. Miller Lite beer, "Tastes great, less filling," McCann-Erickson Worldwide, 1974

9. Clairol, "Does she . . . or doesn't she?" Foote, Cone & Belding, 1957

10. Avis, "We try harder," Doyle Dane Bernbach, 1963

11. Federal Express, "Fast talker," Ally & Gargano, 1982

12. Apple Computer, "1984," Chiat/Day, 1984

13. Alka-Seltzer, "Various ads," Jack Tinker & Partners; Doyle Dane Bernbach; Wells Rich, Greene, 1960s, 1970s

14. Pepsi-Cola, "Pepsi-Cola hits the spot," Newell-Emmett Co., 1940s

15. Maxwell House, "Good to the last drop," Ogilvy, Benson & Mather, 1959

16. Ivory Soap, "99 and 44/100 percent pure," Procter & Gamble Co., 1982

17. American Express, "Do you know me?" Ogilvy & Mather, 1975

18. U.S. Army, "Be all that you can be," N.W. Ayer & Son, 1981

19. Anacin, "Fast, fast, fast relief," Ted Bates & Co., 1952

20. Rolling Stone, "Perception. Reality," Fallon McElligott Rice, 1985

21. Pepsi-Cola, "The Pepsi generation," Batton, Barton, Durstine & Osborn, 1964

22. Hathaway shirts, "The man in the Hathaway shirt," Hewitt, Ogilvy, Benson & Mather, 1951

23. Burma-Shave, "Roadside signs in verse," Allen Odell, 1925

24. Burger King, "Have it your way," BBDO, 1973

25. Campbell Soup, "Mmm, mmm good," BBDO, 1930s

26. U.S. Forest Service, Smokey the Bear, "Only you can prevent forest fires," Advertising Council/Foote, Cone & Belding

27. Budweiser, "This Bud's for you," D'Arcy Masius Benton & Bowles, 1970s

28. Maidenform, "I dreamed I went shopping in my Maidenform bra," Norman, Craig & Kummel, 1949

29. Victor Talking Machine Co., "His master's voice," Francis Barraud, 1901

30. Jordan Motor Car Co., "Somewhere west of Laramie," Edward S. (Ned) Jordan, 1923

31. Woodbury Soap, "The skin you love to touch," J. Walter Thompson Co., 1911

32. Benson & Hedges 100s, "The disadvantages," Wells, Rich, Greene, 1960s

33. National Biscuit Co., "Uneeda Biscuits' Boy in Boots," N.W. Ayer & Son, 1899

34. Energizer, "The Energizer Bunny," Chiat/Day, 1989

35. Morton Salt, "When it rains it pours," N.W. Ayer & Son, 1912

36. Chanel, "Share the fantasy," Doyle Dane Bernbach, 1979

37. Saturn, "A different kind of company. A different kind of car," Hal Riney & Partners, 1989

38. Crest Toothpaste, "Look, Ma! No cavities!" Benton & Bowles, 1958

39. M&Ms, "Melts in your mouth, not in your hands," Ted Bates & Co., 1954

40. Timex, "Takes a licking and keeps on ticking," W.B. Doner & Co & predecessor agencies, 1950s

41. Chevrolet, "See the USA in your Chevrolet," Campbell-Ewald, 1950s

42. Calvin Klein, "Know what comes between me and my Calvins? Nothing!"

43. Reagan for President, "It's morning again in America," Tuesday Team, 1984

44. Winston cigarettes, "Winston tastes good—like a cigarette should," 1954

45. U.S. School of Music, "They laughed when I sat down at the piano, but when I started to play!" Ruthrauff & Ryan, 1925

46. Camel Cigarettes, "I'd walk a mile for a Camel," N. W. Ayer & Son, 1921

47. Wendy's, "Where's the beef?" Dancer-Fitzgerald-Sample, 1984

48. Listerine, "Always a bridesmaid, but never a bride," Lambert & Feasley, 1923

49. Cadillac, "The penalty of leadership," MacManus, John & Adams, 1915

50. Keep America Beautiful, "Crying Indian," Advertising Council/Marstellar Inc., 1971

51. Charmin, "Please don't squeeze the Charmin," Benton & Bowles, 1964

52. Wheaties, "Breakfast of champions," Blackett-Sample-Hummert, 1930s

53. Coca-Cola, "It's the real thing," McCann-Erickson, 1970

54. Greyhound, "It's such a comfort to take the bus and leave the driving to us," Grey Advertising, 1957

55. Kellogg's Rice Krispies, "Snap! Crackle! and Pop!" Leo Burnett Co., 1940s

56. Polaroid, "It's so simple," Doyle Dane Bernbach, 1977

57. Gillette, "Look sharp, feel sharp," BBDO, 1940s

58. Levy's Rye Bread, "You don't have to be Jewish to love Levy's Rye Bread," Doyle Dane Bernbach, 1949

59. Pepsodent, "You'll wonder where the yellow went," Foote, Cone & Belding, 1956

60. Lucky Strike Cigarettes, "Reach for a Lucky instead of a sweet," Lord & Thomas, 1920s

61. 7-Up, "The Uncola," J. Walter Thompson, 1970s

62. Wisk detergent, "Ring around the collar," BBDO, 1968

63. Sunsweet prunes, "Today the pits, tomorrow the wrinkles," Freberg Ltd., 1970s

64. Life cereal, "Hey, Mikey," Doyle Dane Bernbach, 1972

65. Hertz, "Let Hertz put you in the driver's seat," Norman, Craig & Kummel, 1961

66. Foster Grant, "Who's that behind those Foster Grants?" Geer, Dubois, 1965

67. Perdue Chicken, "It takes a tough man to make tender chicken," Scali, McCabe, Sloves, 1971

68. Hallmark, "When you care enough to send the very best," Foote, Cone & Belding, 1930s

69. Springmaid Sheets, "A buck well spent," In-house, 1948

70. Queensboro Corp., "Jackson Heights Apartment Homes," WEAF, NYC, 1920s

71. Steinway & Sons, "The instrument of the immortals," N.W. Ayer & Sons, 1919

72. Levi's Jeans, "501 Blues," Foote, Cone & Belding, 1984

73. Blackglama-Great Lakes Mink, "What becomes a legend most?" Jane Trahey Associates, 1960s

74. Blue Nun Wine, "Stiller & Meara campaign," Della Famina, Travisano & Partners, 1970s

75. Hamm's Beer, "From the land of sky blue waters," Campbell-Mithun, 1950s

76. Quaker Puffed Wheat, "Shot from guns," Lord & Thomas, 1920s

77. ESPN Sports, "This is SportsCenter," Wieden & Kennedy, 1995

78. Molson Beer, "Laughing couple," Moving & Talking Picture Co., 1980s

79. California Milk Processor Board, "Got Milk?," 1993

80. AT&T, "Reach out and touch someone," N.W. Ayer, 1979

81. Brylcreem, "A little dab'll do ya," Kenyon & Eckhardt, 1950s

82. Carling Black Label Beer, "Hey Mabel, Black Label!" Lang, Fisher & Stashower, 1940s

83. Isuzu, "Lying Joe Isuzu," Della Famina, Travisano & Partners, 1980s

84. BMW, "The ultimate driving machine," Ammirati & Puris, 1975

85. Texaco, "You can trust your car to the men who wear the star," Benton & Bowles, 1940s

86. Coca-Cola, "Always," Creative Artists Agency, 1993

87. Xerox, "It's a miracle," Needham, Harper & Steers, 1975

88. Bartles & Jaymes, "Frank and Ed," Hal Riney & Partners, 1985

89. Dannon Yogurt, "Old People in Russia," Marstellar Inc., 1970s

90. Volvo, "Average life of a car in Sweden," Scali, McCabe, Sloves, 1960s

91. Motel 6, "We'll leave a light on for you," Richards Group, 1988

92. Jell-O, "Bill Cosby with kids," Young & Rubicam, 1975

93. IBM, "Chaplin's Little Tramp character," Lord, Geller, Federico, Einstein, 1982

94. American Tourister, "The Gorilla," Doyle Dane Bernbach, late 1960s

95. Right Guard, "Medicine Cabinet," BBDO, 1960s

96. Maypo, "I want my Maypo," Fletcher, Calkins & Holden, 1960s

97. Bufferin, "Pounding heartbeat," Young & Rubicam, 1960

98. Arrow Shirts, "My friend, Joe Holmes, is now a horse," Young & Rubicam, 1938

99. Young & Rubicam, "Impact," Young & Rubicam, 1930

100. Lyndon Johnson for President, "Daisy," Doyle Dane Bernbach, 1964

ELEMENTS OF WEBSITE DESIGN

OU SHOULD EMPHASIZE THESE EIGHT ELEMENTS ON your website:

1. Planning
2. Content
3. Design

4. Involvement
5. Production
6. Follow-up
7. Promotion
8. Maintenance

20 QUESTIONS TO CONSIDER ABOUT YOUR WEBSITE

1. What is the immediate, short-term goal of your website? Be specific.
2. What action do you want visitors to take? Be specific.
3. What are your objectives for the long term? Be specific.
4. Who do you want to visit your site?
5. What solutions or benefits can you offer to these visitors?
6. What data should your site provide to achieve your primary goal?
7. What information can you provide to encourage them to act right now?
8. What questions do you get asked most often on the telephone?
9. What questions and comments do you hear most often at trade shows?
10. What data should your site provide to achieve your long-term objectives?
11. Where does your target audience go for information?
12. How often do you want visitors to return to your website?

13. What may be the reasons you don't sell as much as you'd like to?
14. Who is your most astute competitor?
15. Does your competitor have a website?
16. What are some ways you can distinguish yourself from competitors?
17. How important is price to your target audience?
18. Who is your market?
19. What information does your market need in order to want to take the action you desire?
20. What are you doing to make sure your market visits—and revisits—your website?

Your website will probably be one of your most important marketing tools. Make sure that the site is user-friendly and accomplishes what you want it to by asking yourself these questions.

Does your website:

★ Load quickly?
★ Communicate your area of expertise?
★ Describe the products or services offered?
★ Offer information that will benefit visitors?
★ Describe your unique competitive advantage?
★ Invite visitor participation?
★ Create a sense of professionalism?
★ Establish credibility?

★ Include contact information on every page?

★ State the length and terms of your guarantee or warranty?

★ Provide a pleasant visiting experience?

It's easy to get off track when you are marketing on the internet for the first time. Don't make any of these common mistakes.

12 MOST COMMON MISTAKES MADE WHEN MARKETING ON THE INTERNET

1. Not starting with a plan
2. Falling in love for the wrong reasons
3. Not understanding the power of design
4. Not understanding direct response marketing
5. Not getting it about the power of your email list
6. Not having a traffic generation strategy
7. Not using web 2.0 social media and technology
8. Not using online and offline marketing combinations
9. Failing to track marketing campaigns
10. Thinking you can do it all yourself
11. Failing to create a system
12. Not understanding how technology can help

HEADLINE AND COPYWRITING TIPS

★

For copy ideas, seek knowledge in ten areas

1. Customers
2. Current events
3. Prospects
4. Economic trends
5. Competition

6. Your own offerings
7. Equivalent businesses elsewhere
8. Your community
9. Your own industry
10. Successful advertising

Ten things copy must always be

1. Readable
2. Strategic
3. Motivating
4. Informative
5. Clear
6. Honest
7. Simple
8. Competitive
9. Specific
10. Believable

Embrace these magic words

★ Free
★ New
★ You
★ Sale
★ Introducing
★ Save
★ Money

★ Discover
★ Results
★ Easy
★ Proven
★ Guaranteed
★ Love
★ Benefits

- ★ Alternative
- ★ Now
- ★ Win
- ★ Gain
- ★ Happy
- ★ Trustworthy
- ★ Good-looking
- ★ Comfortable
- ★ Proud
- ★ Healthy
- ★ Sexy
- ★ Safe
- ★ Right
- ★ Security
- ★ Winnings
- ★ Fun
- ★ Value
- ★ Advice
- ★ Wanted
- ★ Announcing
- ★ Your
- ★ People
- ★ Why
- ★ How to

Avoid these tragic words that can undo otherwise fine copy

- ★ Buy
- ★ Obligation
- ★ Failure
- ★ Bad
- ★ Sell
- ★ Loss
- ★ Difficult
- ★ Wrong
- ★ Decision
- ★ Deal
- ★ Liability
- ★ Hard
- ★ Pay
- ★ Death
- ★ Order
- ★ Fail
- ★ Cost
- ★ Worry
- ★ Contract
- ★ Stress
- ★ Must

ABOUT THE AUTHORS

★

JAY **CONRAD LEVINSON** IS THE AUTHOR OF THE BEST-SELLING marketing series in history, *Guerrilla Marketing*, plus over 100 other business books. His books have sold more than 21 million copies worldwide, and his guerrilla concepts have influenced marketing so much that his books appear in 63 languages and are required reading in MBA programs worldwide. Jay taught guerrilla marketing for ten years at the extension division of the University of California in Berkeley. He was a practitioner of it in the United States as senior vice president at J. Walter Thompson, and in Europe as creative director of Leo Burnett Marketing.

A winner of first prizes in all types of media, he was part of the creative teams that made household names of many of the most famous brands in history: The Marlboro Man, The Pillsbury Doughboy, Mr. Clean, Tony the Tiger, Allstate's good hands, United's friendly skies, the Sears Diehard battery, Morris the Cat, and the Jolly Green Giant. He is the chairman of Guerrilla Marketing International.

Jeannie Levinson, his wife, is co-author, mommy of eight, grandma of 27, and great-grandma of 8. She is the president of Guerrilla Marketing International and cofounder of the Guerrilla Marketing Association and the Guerrilla Marketing Business University. She has degrees in nursing, occupational therapy, physical therapy, and architectural drafting. She was also a licensed swimming pool contractor and the sales manager of a national pool company, during which time she was awarded for selling more swimming pools in one year than anyone else in the nation.

Jeannie is a member of The National Association of Professional Women and The National Association of Female Executives. Obviously, she is a guerrilla through and through.

That's why so many people seek her out for advice and guerrilla marketing expertise as a seminar and workshop leader.

She's the co-author of *Guerrilla Creativity*, *Guerrilla Marketing for Free*, *Guerrilla Marketing 4th Edition*, *Startup Guide to Guerrilla Marketing*, and *The Best of Guerrilla Marketing: The Remix*.

Guerrilla marketing is a series of books, workshops, CDs, videos, a website, and The Guerrilla Marketing Association—a marketing support system for small business.

Guerrilla marketing is a way for business owners to spend less, get more, and achieve substantial profits. To receive more information to help you become a guerrilla, go to: www. gmarketing.com.

GUERRILLA ARSENAL

GUERRILLA MARKETING INTERNATIONAL, INC.

Jay Conrad Levinson, Chairman
jayview@aol.com

Jeannie Levinson, President
jeannielevinson@aol.com

Amy Levinson, Executive Vice President
olympiagal@aol.com

www.gmarketing.com
(Main Website—Information, Products, and Services)

Guerrilla Marketing Association

www.guerrillamarketingassociation.com

(Small Business Support Group—Membership Site)

Guerrilla Marketing Business University

(Education: Courses, Seminars, Workshops)

Licensed Guerrilla Marketing Master Trainers

(Representing Guerrilla Marketing Worldwide)

Certified Guerrilla Marketing Coaches

(One on One Coaching)

Guerrilla Marketing Press

(Publishing—Authored & Co-Authored "Guerrilla" Books)

Guerrilla Marketing Network

(Local, Regional, National, and International Conferences)

Guerrilla Marketing On the Go

(Mobile Device Applications)

ENTREPRENEUR BOOKS BY JAY CONRAD LEVINSON

Guerrilla Marketing Remix (with Jeannie Levinson)

Guerrilla Marketing Field Guide (with Jeannie Levinson)

Guerrilla Marketing on the Internet (with Mitch Meyerson and Mary Eule Scarborough)

Guerrilla Social Media Marketing (with Shane Gibson)

Guerrilla Marketing for Nonprofits (with Frank Adkins and Chris Forbes)

Guerrilla Marketing in 30 Days (with Al Lautenslager)

Guerrilla Marketing in 30 Days Workbook (with Al Lautenslager)

Startup Guide to Guerrilla Marketing (with Jeannie Levinson)

GUERRILLA MARKETING PRODUCTS

For information on any Guerrilla Marketing products, please contact Amy Levinson at: olympiagal@aol.com, or by phone: (360) 791-7479, or go to our website: www.gmarketing.com.

INDEX